BELL, BOOK AND CANDLE

Comedy in Three Acts

BY JOHN VAN DRUTEN

★

★

DRAMATISTS
PLAY SERVICE
INC.

Bell, Book and Candle was first presented by Irene Mayer Selznick at the Ethel Barrymore Theater, New York City, on Nov. 14, 1950, with the following cast:

Gillian Holroyd .... Lilli Palmer
Shepherd Henderson .... Rex Harrison
Miss Holroyd .... Jean Adair
Nicky Holroyd .... Scott McKay
Sidney Redlitch .... Larry Gates

Directed by John van Druten

Setting designed by George Jenkins

SCENES

The action passes throughout in Gillian Holroyd's apartment in the Murray Hill district of New York City.

ACT I

Scene 1: Christmas Eve.
Scene 2: About three hours later.

ACT II

Two weeks later.

ACT III

Scene 1: Four hours later.
Scene 2: Two months later.

BELL, BOOK AND CANDLE

◇◇

ACT I

SCENE 1

The scene throughout is Gillian Holroyd's apartment in New York.
It is a first-floor apartment of a converted brownstone house in the
Murray Hill district—the East Thirties.
The living room is interesting and comfortable. There is nothing of
the interior decorator about it. It is a little on the dark side—book-
cases covering one wall and part of another; a number of drawings
and books; a large and comfortable couch. The furniture is good, but
neither modern nor antique: family-looking stuff, mainly, from
Gillian's childhood. Some colored glass, and a witchball or two.
Up R. *there is a swing door to the kitchen, in the* L. *wall a door to*
the bedroom. Below it, an open fireplace with a fire burning. Down
R. *there is an alcove with windows, looking on to the street. The*
front door to the apartment is up C., *and opens straight into the*
room. Small stove below fireplace L.
It is Christmas Eve, about six in the evening. The curtains are open.
There is a Christmas tree, trimmed and lighted, R. *of* C. *door.*
When the curtain rises, GILLIAN *is alone on the stage. She is twenty-*
seven—small, alert, direct, very attractive. She wears a simple and
perhaps slightly arty dinner dress. She is seated on the sofa with a
cat in her arms, stroking and talking to it. She is in the half-dark,
lighted only by the fire and the street lamps through the window.

GILLIAN. (*Talking to cat.*) Oh, Pye—Pye—Pyewacket—what's the
matter with me? Why do I feel this way? It's all such a *rut.* And
you can't get away from it. It was just the same in Mexico. You
know it was. Were the Mexican cats any different from the ones
you know in New York? (*She starts to wander, still carrying the*
cat, to U. C.) Why don't you give me something for Christmas? What
would I like? Well, let's see. I'd like to meet someone *different.* (*She*

5

crosses to back of R. *table.*) Yes, all right. Like the man upstairs, then. (*She looks out of window, then draws back a step, so as not to be seen.*) There he is, coming in now. Did *you* do that? Why don't I ever meet people like that? . . . What's the matter? Want to go out? (*She opens swing door to kitchen.*) All right, then, Pyewacket. There you are. (*She sets cat down in kitchen, returns and lights the liquor console lamp. There is a knock on the door.*) Who's there? (*She switches on the hall light and opens door.* SHEP HENDERSON *is standing outside. He is a man of anywhere from thirty-five up, masculine and attractive. He wears day clothes, a topcoat and carries his hat. He also carries a couple of Christmas-wrapped packages.*)

GILLIAN. Oh . . .

SHEP. (*Steps down to* R. *of her.*) Miss Holroyd?

GILLIAN. Yes.

SHEP. My name's Shepherd Henderson. I live on the floor above. Are you my landlady?

GILLIAN. Yes. How do you do?

SHEP. Are you busy, or could I see you for a moment?

GILLIAN. Certainly. Come in, won't you? (*She closes door.*)

SHEP. Thanks. (*He does so, steps down* R. C.)

GILLIAN. Take off your coat. (*She crosses to sofa table,* L. *and puts on lamp.*)

SHEP. (*Doing so—he crosses to back of* R. *table—puts his hat and packages on it.*) Thanks. I won't keep you long. I imagine you're going out. I am, too. (*Showing packages.*) I've just been getting some last-minute presents I forgot. Well, now . . . (*He steps* L. GILLIAN *crosses to* L.C.)

GILLIAN. (*Interrupting.*) Would you like a drink?

SHEP. I don't think I ought to take time for that. And . . . I don't know that this is an altogether friendly visit . . .

GILLIAN. Oh?

SHEP. You've been away ever since I moved in . . .

GILLIAN. (*Steps toward him.*) Is anything wrong? You should have called the agents.

SHEP. I did. But—well, I'm afraid it doesn't seem to have done much good.

GILLIAN. What's the trouble?

SHEP. The lady on the floor above me. I think she's your aunt.

GILLIAN. Yes?

6

SHEP. Did you ever give her a key to my apartment?

GILLIAN. (*Astonished.*) No, of course not. Why?

SHEP. Well, she's been in it a couple of times. I found her there. And I'm afraid I don't awfully like it.

GILLIAN. No. Naturally. But how did she get in?

SHEP. She said she found the door open. That *may* have been true the first time, though I don't think so. I know it wasn't true, the second. And—even if it were . . .

GILLIAN. (*Shutting up somewhat; something almost guilty about her, as though she knows more than she is saying.*) Oh, I'm sorry. (*She sits on ottoman.*)

SHEP. (*Crossing to back of R. chair. Picks up his packages.*) Yes, well, I thought I'd better tell you, now that you're back.

GILLIAN. (*Worried.*) Yes, of course. Is that all?

SHEP. Isn't it enough?

GILLIAN. (*Laughing, but uncomfortably.*) I didn't mean that. (GILLIAN *gestures to him to sit.* SHEP *puts his packages down, his coat on back of R. chair, and sits.*)

SHEP. Thank you. As a matter of fact, it's *not* really all. I- er—I think your aunt is rather a peculiar lady.

GILLIAN. (*Still worried, and not giving at all.*) Oh?

SHEP. Is she by any chance studying dramatics?

GILLIAN. Dramatics?

SHEP. Well, I can hear her at night through the ceiling, and it sounds as if she were *reciting*—or something.

GILLIAN. (*With obviously embarrassed knowledge.*) Oh.

SHEP. Oh, you know about that? What *is* it that she's doing—or shouldn't I ask?

GILLIAN. Well, it is a *kind* of dramatics. You can't hear what she says?

SHEP. No. And I'm sorry, but there's another thing. Her cooking. At least, again I guess that's what it is. Unless she's an amateur chemist. It doesn't smell like anything I'd be willing to eat.

GILLIAN. It's not cooking. She—she *makes* things. Perfumes and— lotions, and things.

SHEP. It's not *my* idea of perfume. (*Rises, steps to back of chair.*)

GILLIAN. (*Smiles, but still uneasily. Then:*) And that *is* all?

SHEP. (*Half-amused.*) You sound as if you were expecting something worse.

GILLIAN. (*Unconvincingly.*) Oh—No. No. (*She rises, steps to above ottoman.*)

SHEP. (*Stepping* L.) Well, I'm sorry, but there *is* something else. Though I can't be sure it's she who does it.

GILLIAN. What's that?

SHEP. (*Crossing to* c.) Well, ever since I caught her in my place—and talked to the agents about it—rather firmly, I'm afraid—I imagine they spoke to *her*—my telephone's started ringing at eight o'clock every morning—and around midnight, too—and when I answer it, there's no one there. I've talked to the telephone company, but they can't trace anything.

GILLIAN. And you think it's Aunt Queenie?

SHEP. I've no *proof* that that is. But—well . . .

GILLIAN. (*With decision, frankly.*) Mr. Henderson, I'm most awfully sorry. I'll talk to Aunt Queenie. She *is* a little—eccentric, but I promise you none of this will happen again.

SHEP. *Can* you promise?

GILLIAN. Yes. I can. I really can.

SHEP. (*Smiles.*) Well, thanks, then. I don't mean to be unpleasant. . . .

GILLIAN. I'm only sorry I've not been here before.

SHEP. (*Crosses to back of* R. *table, picking up his coat, hat and packages.*) You've been traveling about, I understand.

GILLIAN. Yes, I've been in Haiti, and Mexico.

SHEP. (*Stepping to back of* R. *chair.*) Whereabouts in Mexico?

GILLIAN. (*Stepping up* c.) I had a house in Taxco.

SHEP. (*Crossing to* c.) Oh—you didn't, by any chance, run into Redlitch down there, did you? The man who wrote that book on magic. *Magic in Mexico.*

GILLIAN. (*Steps upstage.*) No, he'd left by the time I got there. (*Rather searchingly.*) Why—are you interested in that sort of thing?

SHEP. Not personally—but professionally. I'm a publisher.

GILLIAN. Did you publish his book?

SHEP. No, but I wish I had. It sold like the Kinsey Report.

GILLIAN. I can't think why.

SHEP. (*Shrugging.*) It was sensational.

GILLIAN. And completely phony. They fed him a whole lot of fake tourist staff, and he swallowed it whole. (*She crosses to* R. *of sofa.*)

SHEP. Maybe they did that to Kinsey, too. (THEY *laugh.*) But I heard that Redlitch was ready to change publishers, and I'd kind of like his next one. I've written to him several times, but I got no answer.

GILLIAN. (*Eagerly—steps toward him.*) If you'd like to meet him . . .

SHEP. (*Stepping up* c.) Oh, do you know him?

8

GILLIAN. No, but I know people who do. I can arrange it.

SHEP. I'd appreciate that, very much. (*Starting out.*) Well, I'll get along.

GILLIAN. (*Following him.*) Won't you have that drink now? There are some Martinis in the kitchen.

SHEP. I mustn't. I'm late. But—if I may have a raincheck . . .

GILLIAN. Yes, of course. And I'll have Redlitch here to meet you.

SHEP. (*Crossing to her, shakes her hand.*) That would be fine. I hear he's a drunk and a nut, but . . . (*Looking at a drawing on the wall.*) Say, that's kind of interesting. Who did that?

GILLIAN. My brother.

SHEP. He's good. Ought I to know his stuff?

GILLIAN. I don't think so. Nicky's very lazy.

SHEP. (*Looking at drawing again. Picks it up and turns front.*) It's a strange face. Who is it, do you know?

GILLIAN. (*After a half beat's pause.*) It's a Brazilian girl who used to dance in a night club here. (*She crosses down to R. of sofa.*) A place called the Zodiac.

SHEP. (*Looking at her.*) I don't know it.

GILLIAN. I don't imagine you would.

SHEP. Why not?

GILLIAN. Oh, because—well, it's a sort of—*dive.*

SHEP. (*Smiling.*) But *you* know it?

GILLIAN. I've *been* there. . . .

SHEP. Well . . . (*A knock on the door.*) You've got visitors. I must be getting along. (*He replaces drawing.* GILLIAN *goes to door.* MISS HOLROYD *is outside. She is an odd-looking woman, vague, fluttery and eccentric. She is dressed in a wispy evening gown, bitty and endy, with a trailing scarf, bangles and a long necklace. When she talks it is in a high, feathery voice, with a trilling little laugh. She carries her cloak, and three gift-wrapped packages.*)

GILLIAN. Oh, Aunt Queenie . . .

MISS HOLROYD. (*Comes in.*) Hello, darling. Merry . . . (*She stops on seeing* SHEP, *and with embarrassment crosses* L.) Oh, I didn't know you had company.

GILLIAN. (*Closing door.*) It's all right. This is . . . (*Then, with some meaning.*) Oh, yes . . . you know each other.

SHEP. (*Amused, friendly.*) Hello, Miss Holroyd.

MISS HOLROYD. (*Formally.*) How do you do?

SHEP. (*Starting to leave.*) Well . . .

MISS HOLROYD. Don't let me drive you away.

9

SHEP. I have to go. (*Crosses up to door*—GILLIAN *opens it.*) SHEP *holds out his hand to* GILLIAN.) Well, good night, and—Merry Christmas.

GILLIAN. (*Taking his hand.*) And to you.

SHEP. Thank you. (*Bowing to* MISS HOLROYD.) Good night. (GILLIAN *closes door, crosses to* U.L. *of ottoman.* MISS HOLROYD *walks away with exaggerated nonchalance, aware of the scolding that is coming to her, and trying only to postpone it. She puts her cape on window seat and presents on* R. *table.* GILLIAN *stands watching her, like a cat waiting to pounce.*)

MISS HOLROYD. So you've met him, after all. Do you still think he's attractive?

GILLIAN. (*Quietly.*) Yes, I do. Very.

MISS HOLROYD. (*Crossing to back of* R. *chair.*) Did you—bring him here?

GILLIAN. No. He came here to talk to me. (*Pause. Then, springing it. She turns to* MISS HOLROYD.) About *you.*

MISS HOLROYD. (*Naïvely.*) Me?

GILLIAN. (*Coming toward her.*) Yes, and it's no good acting innocent. I'm angry. *Really* angry.

MISS HOLROYD. (*Backing to* R. *of table.*) Why, what have I done?

GILLIAN. (*Above* R. *table.*) You know. Broken into his apartment—played tricks with his telephone . . .

MISS HOLROYD. That was because he reported me to the agents. (*She backs to below* R. *chair.*) That was just to pay him out.

GILLIAN. (*Very angry, she crosses to below table.*) I don't care *what* it was. You *promised* when I let you move in here . . .

MISS HOLROYD. I promised to be careful.

GILLIAN. And do you call that being careful? Getting caught in his apartment? Twice!

MISS HOLROYD. What harm did I do? I didn't *take* anything. (*She crosses to* C.) Oh, yes, I read his letters, it's not as if I were going to make *use* of them. Though I'm tempted to now—now that he's told on me—to you. (*She steps* R.)

GILLIAN. (*Menacingly, and quite frighteningly.*) Auntie, if you do —well, you'll be sorry. And you know I can *make* you sorry, too.

MISS HOLROYD. (*Defensively. She sits in* R. *chair.* GILLIAN *steps to* R. *of table.*) He'd never suspect, darling. Not in a million years. No matter *what* I did. Honestly, it's amazing the way people don't. Why, they don't believe there *are* such things. I sit in the subway sometimes, or in busses, and look at the people next to me, and I think: I wonder what you would say if I told you I was a witch? They'd never believe it. I just know they wouldn't believe it. And I giggle and giggle to myself.

GILLIAN. (*Crossing to above* R. *table,* L. *of* MISS HOLROYD.) Well, you've got to stop giggling here. You've got to swear, swear on the Manual . . .

MISS HOLROYD. (*Retreating a step, to below table.*) Swear what?

GILLIAN. (*Crossing to above ottoman, turns to her.*) That you'll stop practicing—in this house—ever.

MISS HOLROYD. *You* practice here.

GILLIAN. I can be discreet about it. You can't.

MISS HOLROYD. (*Very hurt. She crosses down* R.) I shall move to a hotel.

GILLIAN. Very well. But if you get into trouble there, don't look to *me* to get you out.

MISS HOLROYD. (*Huffily.*) I've other people I can turn to.

GILLIAN. (*Scornfully.*) Mrs. de Pass, I suppose.

MISS HOLROYD. Yes, she's done a lot for me.

GILLIAN. (*Crosses up.* L.) Well, I wouldn't count on Mrs. de Pass, if *I* turn against you. I'm a lot better than *that* old phony. Now . . . (*She gets a large white-bound book from a closet—in book-case.*)

MISS HOLROYD. (*Really scared.*) Oh, Gillian, please—not on the Manual.

GILLIAN. (*Crosses down* C.L. *of ottoman. Relentlessly.*) On the Manual. (MISS HOLROYD *crosses to* GILLIAN.) Now, put your hand on it. (MISS HOLROYD *does so, terrified.*) Now, then, I swear that I will not practice witchcraft in this house ever again. So help me Tagla, Salamandrae, Brazo and Vesturiel. Say, "I swear."

MISS HOLROYD. (*After a moment.*) I swear.

GILLIAN. Good. (*She replaces book.*)

MISS HOLROYD. I think you're very cruel. (*She crosses to below sofa.*)

GILLIAN. (*Returning, somewhat softened, to* R. *of sofa.*) Oh, Auntie, if you'd only have a little sense!

MISS HOLROYD. (*Continuing.*) *And* hypocritical. Sometimes I think you're ashamed of being what you are. (*She sits* C. *of sofa.*)

GILLIAN. Ashamed? I'm not in the least ashamed. No, it's not a question of that, but . . . (*Sits on arm of sofa.*) Auntie, don't you ever wish you *weren't?*

MISS HOLROYD. (*Amazed.*) No!

GILLIAN. That you were like those people you sit next to in the busses?

MISS HOLROYD. Ordinary and humdrum? No, I *was*. For years. Before I came into it.

GILLIAN. Well, you came in late. And, anyway, I don't *mean* humdrum. I just mean unenlightened. And I don't hanker for it all the time. Just sometimes.

MISS HOLROYD. (*Patting* GILLIAN's *arm.*) Darling, you're depressed . . .

GILLIAN. I know. I expect it's Christmas. It's always upset me.

MISS HOLROYD. You wait till you get to Zoe's party, and see all your old friends again.

GILLIAN. (*Crossing to above* R. *table.*) I don't *want* to see all my old friends again. I want something different.

MISS HOLROYD. (*Moves* R. *on sofa.*) Well, come with me to Mrs. de Pass's, then. She's got some very interesting people. Some French people. From the Paris chapter.

GILLIAN. (*Laughing. Turns to her—crosses to below table.*) I didn't mean *that*, when I said I wanted something different. No, I think maybe I'd like to spend the evening with some everyday people for a change, instead of us.

MISS HOLROYD. (*Archly.*) With Mr. Henderson?

GILLIAN. I wouldn't mind.

MISS HOLROYD. It's too bad he's getting married. Still, I suppose . . .

GILLIAN. *He's* getting married? (*She crosses to ottoman.*)

MISS HOLROYD. Yes, quite soon. They're going to announce it New Year's Eve.

GILLIAN. How do you know that? Oh, the telephone, I suppose.

MISS HOLROYD. Yes, dear.

GILLIAN. Who's he getting married to? Do you know?

MISS HOLROYD. I don't know her last name. Her first name's Merle.

GILLIAN. Merle? The only Merle I ever knew was a girl I was in college with. (*Sitting on ottoman.*) Merle Kittredge. She used to write poison-pen letters. I caught her writing one about me, once. That's why we had all those thunderstorms that spring. She was terrified of them. (*Smiling at the recollection.*) We had one every day for a month. It was most extraordinary.

MISS HOLROYD. You mean that that was *you?* (*Delighted.*) Oh, Gillian, you were naughty!

GILLIAN. (*Crosses up to* L. *of Christmas tree.*) She was a nervous wreck by the end of the term.

MISS HOLROYD. And you think this might be the same girl? What was she like?

GILLIAN. (*Leaning against* R. *pillar*.) Southern, and blonde, and helpless . . .

MISS HOLROYD. This one's blonde. He's got her picture on his bureau.

GILLIAN. (*Continuing her catalogue*.) And appealing. And underneath, a liar and a sneak and a beau-snatcher.

MISS HOLROYD. Did you ever hear what happened to her?

GILLIAN. I think she became a decorator.

MISS HOLROYD. This one's a decorator.

GILLIAN. Oh!—(*She crosses down* C. *After a moment's pause*.) Well, there's probably more than one decorator in New York called Merle. And, if he's engaged, that rules him out. (*Crossing to below console*.)

MISS HOLROYD. I don't see why.

GILLIAN. I'm not a Southern belle. I don't take other women's men. (*Steps downstage*.) Though I would, if it *were* Merle Kittredge.

MISS HOLROYD. I could find out for you.

GILLIAN. (*Crosses to back of* R. *chair, leans on it*.) But—New Year's. That wouldn't leave me much time.

MISS HOLROYD. You wouldn't *need* time. Just a quick little potion. Or—four words to Pyewacket, you once told me.

GILLIAN. Yes, but I wouldn't want him that way. That would take the challenge out of it. Especially with her. Other girls can make men like them in a week. Why can't I?

MISS HOLROYD. Did he seem to like you this afternoon?

GILLIAN. (*With rueful humor*.) Not very much. No. (*Crosses to* R. *of table*.)

MISS HOLROYD. (*With sudden alarm. She rises and crosses to ottoman*.) Gillian, you—you haven't fallen in love with him, and lost your powers, have you? That isn't what this is all about?

GILLIAN. (*Laughing*.) No, of course not.

MISS HOLROYD. Oh, thank goodness! (*She sits on ottoman*.)

GILLIAN. (*Crossing to up* R. *of ottoman*.) You don't *believe* that old wives' tale?

MISS HOLROYD. Of course I do! It's true. They say it's true.

GILLIAN. (*Crossing* L. *of ottoman, down* C. *to coffee table*.) It's the other way around. We can't fall in love. (*Pause*.) Merle Kittredge. I haven't thought of her in years. (*Pause again. She sits on* R. *end of coffee table*.) Do you think—if it were she—I could do it in a week—without tricks?

MISS HOLROYD. Darling, it's no good asking me. I never could do it at all. But if it is, why don't you pull a quick one, and have done with it?

GILLIAN. No. I don't say I wouldn't be tempted, but if I've got a week—I'd like to see how good I am, the other way. (*The buzzer sounds. She answers it, unhooking mouthpiece.*) Hello?

NICKY'S VOICE. (*In mouthpiece.*) It's me. Nicky.

GILLIAN. Good. (*She buzzes and hangs up.*) I'll get the drinks. (*She goes into kitchen.* MISS HOLROYD *looks after her—goes to the telephone and stands for a moment with her hand on receiver, as though to make a call. Then she thinks better of it. Front door opens and* NICKY *comes in. He is* GILLIAN'*s brother, a little younger, and has an engaging, impish and somewhat impertinent personality. He wears a dark suit, topcoat, and carries some small Christmas-wrapped packages.*)

MISS HOLROYD. (*She crosses to him,* C.) Nicky, dear!

NICKY. (*Steps down* L., *after closing door.*) Hello, Auntie. Merry Christmas. (*He kisses her.*) Where's Gill?

MISS HOLROYD. In the kitchen. (*Looking over her shoulder, and speaking low.*) Nicky, will you do something for me?

NICKY. (*Takes off his coat, puts it on* L. *bench in archway, crosses to her.*) Sure. What?

MISS HOLROYD. Have you got a pencil and paper? Never mind! (*Sees block by telephone, and crosses to it, back of sofa table.*) Oh, this will do. (*She writes on it, tears off sheet.*) Nicky, this number, I want you to fix it for me.

NICKY. (*Crosses to her and puts his packages on table.*) Fix it?

MISS HOLROYD. *You* know. (*Gives him paper.*)

NICKY. Why, who is it?

MISS HOLROYD. (*Crossing below him, to up* R. *of* R. *chair.*) Someone I want to—pay back for something.

NICKY. (*Crossing* C., *above ottoman.*) But you can pull that one for yourself. I taught you.

MISS HOLROYD. (*Crossing to him.*) Yes, but I just had to promise Gillian that I wouldn't in this house any more. So will you do it for me?

NICKY. Anything to oblige.

MISS HOLROYD. Hurry, dear! (*She crosses, sits on window seat.*)

NICKY. (*He goes to telephone, lifts receiver, holds down bar and begins to mutter.*) Actatus, Catipta, Itapan, Marnutus. (GILLIAN *returns with a pitcher of Martinis.* MISS HOLROYD *looks out the window.*) Murray Hill 6-4476. (*He hangs up.*) Hello, darling.

GILLIAN. (*Watching* NICKY.) What are you two up to? (*Warningly, turns to* MISS HOLROYD.) Auntie . . .

MISS HOLROYD. (*Innocently turning to her.*) I haven't done a thing.

GILLIAN. Whose number was that you were fixing?

NICKY. (*Putting paper in his pocket and crosses* C.) No one you know, dear.

GILLIAN. (*Crosses to console, puts Martini pitcher on it.*) Just a little Christmas present for a friend? No telephone for a week? (*Crossing to him,* C., *embraces him.*) Oh, Nicky, when will you grow up? How are you?

NICKY. Fine. (THEY *kiss.*) Merry Christmas, darling.

GILLIAN. Pour the drinks, will you, and then we'll have presents. (*She goes to tree, takes two packages, then crosses to sofa and sits* C.)

NICKY. (*Goes to liquor console.*) I'm afraid mine's pretty mingy, dear—but I've never been more broke. You know, I used to wonder when I was a kid why all the witches in history were always poor and miserable old men and women, living in hovels, when you'd have thought they could have anything they wanted. But I've learned why, since. (*He gives a drink to* MISS HOLROYD *at window.*)

MISS HOLROYD. (*Rises.*) It's only because they weren't *good* enough at it. Any more than *we* are.

NICKY. (*Crossing with drink to sofa.*) Or else they got scared, like Gill here. (*Giving* GILLIAN *her glass, then going back to liquor console.*) She admitted to me once that she could hex the whole Stock Market if she wanted. (*Picks up his drink.*)

MISS HOLROYD. (*Crosses to* R. *of* R. *table.*) Oh, Gillian, could you? Really, dear? Why don't you do it?

NICKY. (*Crossing* C. *above ottoman.*) She said she was afraid of the repercussions.

GILLIAN. I didn't say that, at all. Nicky, you still don't know what this kind of thing can do to you—if you go too far. (*Then, breaking off.*) But that's nothing to talk about tonight. (*Rises, raising her glass.*) Merry Christmas.

MISS HOLROYD AND NICKY. Merry Christmas. (ALL *drink.*)

GILLIAN. (*Puts her drink on coffee table.*) Now. (*Crossing to Nicky, gives him records.*) Nicky. Aunt Queenie—(*Crossing to back of* R. *table.*)

MISS HOLROYD. (*Bringing her two packages.*) For you, darling. And for Nicky. (*Crossing* C.)

NICKY. (*Doing likewise.*) Auntie. Gillian. (*He crosses back to up* C. THEY *start to open their packages.*)

MISS HOLROYD. (*Crossing to below sofa, sits.*) You two are the hardest people to find presents for. I gave you both the same thing.

GILLIAN. (*At L. of R. chair. Opening hers.*) A book.

NICKY. (*Looking at his.*) *Magic in Mexico*, by Sidney Redlitch.

MISS HOLROYD. They're autographed.

GILLIAN. (*Steps down to L. of R. chair.*) Why—do you know him?

MISS HOLROYD. No, but Mrs. de Pass does. She got them for me.

NICKY. (*Sits on ottoman, puts wrappings and book under it.*) Well, thank you very much. I've heard a lot about it.

MISS HOLROYD. I hope you haven't read it.

GILLIAN. (*Gets MISS HOLROYD's glass, crosses to her and kisses her.*) I have. But I'm very glad to have it. Thank you, Auntie. Here's your drink. (*Crosses to sofa table, puts her gifts on it, takes her cocktail, crosses to NICKY who is unwrapping records.*) Careful with those, Nicky. Those are records.

NICKY. Oh, fine. Only . . . (*Ruefully.*) I don't have a phonograph any more.

GILLIAN. (*Smiling, crosses U.R. of NICKY.*) I think you'll find you have, when you get home.

NICKY. Oh, darling—no! You shouldn't.

GILLIAN. Why not?

NICKY. It's so extravagant. Or did you . . . (*With a gesture.*) "get" it for me? Was it witched, or paid for?

GILLIAN. (*Smiling.*) None of your business.

NICKY. I know. But tell me.

GILLIAN. (*As before, teasingly.*) I will not. (*She crosses to console, puts down her drink. Steps to R. table, and picks up gift from NICKY.*)

MISS HOLROYD. (*Severely.*) You shouldn't ask that, Nicky. It's like asking what it cost!

NICKY. Thanks all the same, darling—either way. (*Inspecting records.*) What *are* these?

GILLIAN. (*Crossing L., to him.*) A man at a party in Mexico. We took some recordings of the incantations.

NICKY. Oh, wonderful. What are they for?

GILLIAN. (*Smiling, crossing down L. below coffee table.*) Try them and see. You'll be surprised. Like to have music come out of your ears?

NICKY. No?

GILLIAN. That's the least of them. (*Crosses to L. of sofa.*)

NICKY. I'll take them to Natalie's party with me. Think they'll help me make any headway with her?

GILLIAN. (*Amused.*) Well, the man had quite a way with him. He had a mink as his familiar.

MISS HOLROYD. (*Unwrapping an elaborate lace mantilla.*) Oh, how sweet! Where did you find this? Oh, this is lovely, darling. Simply lovely. (*She puts it on.*) What does it *do*? (NICKY *crosses up to sofa,* R.)

GILLIAN. It makes you look fascinating.

MISS HOLROYD. (*Hopefully, she poses.*) You mean . . . ?

GILLIAN. (*Smiling.*) No, Auntie, I'm afraid it has no powers. I just thought it was pretty. (*She crosses down to* L. *of coffee table.*)

MISS HOLROYD. (*Very disappointed, takes it off, folds it.*) Oh, it is. Very pretty. I love it.

NICKY. (*To* GILLIAN.) Why didn't you say it had powers, and that you wouldn't tell her what they were? Then she'd have had such fun wearing it, and trying to find out.

MISS HOLROYD. (*Severely, as before.*) Gillian doesn't tell lies—*ever.*

NICKY. No, but she manages to hold out plenty! (*He hands her a small bottle, sits next to her.*) Here's something that has got powers for you, Auntie. It's an unguent. You feel colors. Quite a sensation. (*Teasing her.*) Kind of sexy, too. (SHE *giggles. Then, to* GILLIAN, *as she unwraps small phial.*) I got that in a new little shop I've found. It's a sort of paint. For summoning. You just paint it on an image—or a drawing or a photograph, they said—of anyone you want, and then set light to it. And they have to come. (*He rises, backs* R.) I hope it works for you. *I* couldn't even make it light. Try it. Now.

GILLIAN. Whom do we want here?

MISS HOLROYD. (*Archly.*) Him! (*She points to ceiling.*)

GILLIAN. No, *I* know. (*She crosses up* L., *back of sofa table, picks up book.*)

NICKY. Who? (*Crosses up to* R. *of* GILLIAN.)

GILLIAN. (*Holding up Redlitch's book.*) This man.

NICKY. Redlitch? What on earth for?

GILLIAN. I want to meet him. I've promised to introduce him to somebody. I thought I'd find someone who knew him, but this will save a lot of time. It's got his picture on the back. Auntie, you don't mind if I cut it off?

MISS HOLROYD. Not if I can stay and watch.

GILLIAN. (*Crossing* R., *getting scissors from desk drawer.*) How soon is it supposed to work? (*She cuts picture on jacket.*)

NICKY. (*Crossing to* GILLIAN.) Depends on how far they've got to come. But within twenty-four hours, nowadays, anyway, I should think. You don't have to stay home, if that's what you're worried about. He'll probably turn up at your party tonight.

GILLIAN. (*Who has cut out picture, crosses* L., *sits sofa.*) Good! put out the lights, Nicky, will you? (NICKY *puts out console lamp, hall light and sofa lamp. Again the room is lighted by the fire and the street-lamp.*)

GILLIAN. Auntie, the big ashtray. (MISS HOLROYD *crosses to back of sofa table, gets ashtray and brings it to* GILLIAN, *then sits* L. *of her.*)

NICKY. (*Up* C.) There's a little brush in the cork.

GILLIAN. I've found it. (*She smears paint on picture.*) Any words?

NICKY. (*Crossing to* R. *of coffee table, kneels.*) They said not.

GILLIAN. All right, then. Got a match? (NICKY *produces one.*)

NICKY. Go. (SHE *touches a match to the picture, which she has placed in ashtray. It goes up in blue flame.* MISS HOLROYD *squeals.*)

NICKY. You're a marvel. (*There is a knock on the door,* HE *rises.*) Not *already?* Gill, that's genius!

GILLIAN. (*Laughing.*) No, of course it isn't. Go and see who it is. (NICKY *opens door.* SHEP *is standing outside. He has changed into a dinner jacket, wears a dark topcoat, and carries a carton filled with presents.*)

NICKY. Yes?

SHEP. Is Miss Holroyd in?

GILLIAN. Oh . . . Mr. Henderson—come in. (*She rises, switching on sofa table lamp.* NICKY *closes door, steps to below tree table.*)

SHEP. (*Crossing to above ottoman.*) I'm sorry if I'm disturbing you. Are you having indoor fireworks?

GILLIAN. Oh—no—no, it's just some nonsense that my brother gave me. This is my brother, Mr. Henderson.

SHEP AND NICKY. (THEY *shake hands.*) How do you do?

SHEP. Please go on with what you were doing.

GILLIAN. It's all right. We'd finished. Really. (*She places cup over flame in tray, smothering it.*) (*She crosses up to* SHEP.) Is there something I can do for you?

SHEP. I just wondered if I might use your telephone? Mine's really turned into a problem child. It's gone right out of order.

GILLIAN. (*With a quick look at* MISS HOLROYD *and* NICKY, *who evade her eyes.* NICKY *crosses to console, puts on lamp.*) Of course. Help yourself.

SHEP. Well, thank you. (*He sets down carton on* R. *hall bench, and goes to phone, talking while he does so and while he dials.* GILLIAN *turns accusingly to* MISS HOLROYD, *who hurries to her cloak, on window seat.*)

MISS HOLROYD. I really must be going! (NICKY *helps her with cloak.*)

SHEP. I used mine right after I left here, and it was doing fine. Then, for the last fifteen minutes, I've been getting nothing but a lot of hiccups in my ear. Busy. May I wait just a minute? (*Hangs up.*)

GILLIAN. (*Up* C.) Of course. Maybe you'd like to report your line?

SHEP. Oh, thanks. (*He dials O.*)

GILLIAN. (*Crossing* R., *to* NICKY.) Nicky, that piece of paper you put in your pocket? I'd like to see it for a minute. (*She holds out her hand for it.* NICKY *gives it to her.*)

SHEP. (*Into phone.*) Hello, Operator? I want to report a line out of order. Murray Hill 6-4476. (GILLIAN *receives paper from* NICKY *and compares numbers, simultaneously with this. Then crosses to* MISS HOLROYD.) I don't know. I can't get a dialing tone.

MISS HOLROYD. (*Seeing* GILLIAN's *face.*) It was Nicky.

GILLIAN. I know.

MISS HOLROYD. (*Smiling, archly.*) But I think it's worked out wonderfully.

SHEP. If you would. Thanks. (*He hangs up.*)

MISS HOLROYD. (*Crossing* L. *below* GILLIAN.) Well, good-by. And . . . (*With a playful glance at* SHEP's *back.*) Good luck.

NICKY. (*Crossing to up* C.) Well, good-bye, Mr. Henderson. I'm glad to have met you.

SHEP. Me, too. (THEY *shake hands.* SHEP *crosses up* L. *to stove, lights cigarette.*)

NICKY. (*Crosses to above ottoman. To* GILLIAN) Can I leave these records here? I'm going to a cocktail party first, and I don't want them to get broken. You know, under all the coats on the bed. I'll pick them up on my way to Natalie's.

GILLIAN. (*Back of* R. *chair.*) I won't be here.

NICKY. (*Steps to her.*) I can get in.

GILLIAN. (*Dubiously.*) Oh—well, all right, then. (NICKY *crosses up to hall, gets his coat.*)

MISS HOLROYD. (*Indignantly stepping to* GILLIAN.) Well, really, if Nicky can, I . . .

GILLIAN. (*Amused.*) I know, Auntie. It's not fair. It's not a bit fair. (*Takes* MISS HOLROYD *up* C.) Take her away, Nicky.

MISS HOLROYD. (*Put out, crosses down to ottoman.*) Good-bye, Mr. Henderson. I hope your telephone gets well, soon. (NICKY *and* MISS HOLROYD *leave.* NICKY *closes door.*)

SHEP. (*Going back to phone.*) I'll just try once more, and then I'll go, too.

GILLIAN. (*Crossing below ottoman, to coffee table, picks up cocktail glasses.*) There's no hurry.

SHEP. (*Dialing.*) You're going out, aren't you?

GILLIAN. Later. But it's not important . . . (*She crosses to console.*)

SHEP. (*Getting his number.*) Ah—luck! (GILLIAN *starts for kitchen with Martini pitcher.*) You don't have to go.

GILLIAN. I'll be back.

SHEP. (*Into phone.*) Hello . . . Is Miss Kittredge there? (GILLIAN *hears this, registers it, then goes into kitchen.*) Merle? It's me. I got delayed. I tried to get you, but the phone's gone off again. (*He takes phone, crosses down to* R. *of sofa, and sets phone base on coffee table.*) Darling, they're fed up with my complaints by now. I'm getting a taxi in two shakes, but . . . What? Oh, darling, won't you mind? Really? Well, that's wonderful, bless you. I'll meet you there, then. What is it? (GILLIAN *returns with shaker, refilled with Martinis.* HE *sits on* R. *arm.*) What's your idea? Tonight? Announce it tonight? Well, wonderful. I thought you were so keen on New Year's Eve. Well, that's fine. Let's tell them all. (GILLIAN, *having registered this, too, returns to kitchen.*) Yes, I've got everything. All the presents. Yours, theirs, everybody's. Yes, darling, I've got that, too, though why you want it, I can't think. Sure. O.K. (GILLIAN *returns again, carrying cat.*) Fifteen minutes. I can't wait. Good-bye, darling. Darling! (*He hangs up. Turns and sees* GILLIAN, *who moves to* R. *chair, where she sits nursing cat.*) Oh . . . I didn't hear you come back. (*He puts phone back on* R. *end of sofa table.*) Is that your cat? I've seen him on the stairs here lately, watching me come in and out. What's his name? (*He crosses to her.*)

GILLIAN. Pyewacket.

SHEP. How's that?

GILLIAN. Pyewacket.

SHEP. (*Trying to shake hands with cat.*) How do you do? Ouch!

GILLIAN. Did he scratch you?

SHEP. (*Finger in mouth.*) No, he didn't make it.

GILLIAN. (*Slaps cat lightly and playfully.*) Bad cat.

SHEP. (*Moving as though to say good-bye.*) Well, I've bothered you enough . . .

GILLIAN. Won't you have that drink now?

SHEP. (*Steps downstage.*) Thanks. I know it must sound as if I were trying to duck it. I'm not—really—but I am late and—tonight's kind of an important night. So, if you don't mind . . .

GILLIAN. No, of course not.

SHEP. Thanks all the same. Well . . . (*He crosses up to* R. *hall bench, puts on his muffler, and lifts the carton, and his hat, with his back to her.* SHE *goes on stroking cat.*)

GILLIAN. Pye - Pye - Pyewacket—this is Mr. Henderson. Mr. Shepherd Henderson. (*She goes on stroking, and mutters quietly, rhythmically.*) Reterrem, Salibat, Cratares, Hisaster.

SHEP. (*Turning, steps downstage.*) What was that?

GILLIAN. I was talking to the cat. I think he wants to go out. (*She rises, avoiding his eye, and goes into kitchen.* SHEP *stands for a moment still holding carton, staring after her. Then crosses down to above ottoman. She comes back, without cat. She holds his eye. She takes a few steps into the room, then stops above* R. *chair.* SHEP *takes two steps forward, then sets down carton on ottoman, his hat on carton, then his muffler, and moves toward her.* SHE *takes a step toward him—then they are in each other's arms.*)

CURTAIN

ACT I

SCENE 2

The same. About two hours later.

When the curtain rises, GILLIAN *and* SHEP *are on the couch. He is reclining, his legs crossed. She is leaning against him, with his arm around her. The room is darker than it was—the curtains are drawn —only one lamp is on, lighting the couch.* SHEP's *hat, coat and muffler are thrown on carton. The carton is on the window seat.* GILLIAN's *jacket is above carton. The door to the bedroom is partly open.*

SHEP. (*After a long moment.*) Say something.

GILLIAN. What?

SHEP. Anything. It doesn't matter. I just want to hear your voice again.

GILLIAN. Do you like my voice?

SHEP. No. (*She looks up, surprised.*) I don't like anything about you. I'm just—*insane* over you. All of you. You should know that, by now. Don't you?

GILLIAN. Well . . .

SHEP. Well . . . Don't you?

GILLIAN. (*With a satisfied smile.*) Well, you made it charmingly apparent. (SHEP *kisses her—a long silence of sheer contentment falls on them.*)

SHEP. You know, there's a wonderful, suspended, *timeless* feeling to this moment, and the two of us like this. I feel—spellbound.

GILLIAN. (*Quietly.*) Stay that way.

SHEP. I don't ever want to move. (*Another pause.*) What are you thinking?

GILLIAN. Nothing. Not a thing. And you?

SHEP. Nothing, either. I can't think. Certainly not this close to you. I've got to start soon, though. Very soon. (*He rises, crosses up L, back of sofa table to c.*)

GILLIAN. What about?

SHEP. (*Grimly.*) A lot of things. (*He goes to console.*) I think I'd better have myself a drink. Can I fix you one?

GILLIAN. (*Leaning back on sofa.*) No, thanks. (*He turns on lamp and mixes himself a highball.* SHE *watches him, stilly, rather like a cat. He drinks, then looks at his watch—steps L., puts watch to his ear to see that it is still going, and amazed, crosses c.*)

SHEP. Do you happen to know what time it is?

GILLIAN. No.

SHEP. It's ten o'clock. A good three hours since I came in here. Since I went to that door to leave.

GILLIAN. Well?

SHEP. Doesn't that seem strange to you?

GILLIAN. Not strange . . . It—happened . . .

SHEP. Nothing like this has ever happened to me before.

GILLIAN. Do you mind?

SHEP. I *ought* to mind. . . .

GILLIAN. Why?

SHEP. In the first place, I was on my way to a party.

GILLIAN. And you found something you'd rather do.

SHEP. (*Crossing toward her.*) That, my girl, is an understatement. I found something I couldn't resist doing.

GILLIAN. (*Smiling.*) You don't have to explain to me.

SHEP. It's fantastic. (*He comes back to sofa, sets down his drink, sits on R. arm of sofa, taking her hands.*) Gillian—tell me—just what has it meant to you?

22

GILLIAN. Meant?

SHEP. These three hours.

GILLIAN. They've been—enchantment.

SHEP. And that's all?

GILLIAN. What more?

SHEP. I don't know. I know it doesn't make sense, but somewhere, I've got an idea—that I must be in love with you. . . . Are you—at all in love with me?

GILLIAN. I like you more than I can say.

SHEP. Yes—well, that wasn't what I asked you.

GILLIAN. Do we have to talk about it?

SHEP. Yes. I've got to know.

GILLIAN. Why?

SHEP. Because I've got to face a few decisions.

GILLIAN. Now?

SHEP. (*Rises and crosses to up* R.C.) I should think so. There are people waiting for me—wondering where the hell I am. There's a whole future that's either got completely shot to hell, or else—well, I've got to do some fast talking. (*Crossing back to sofa.*) And I'd like to know where I stand. Where *we* stand.

GILLIAN. What do you want to do?

SHEP. (*Slowly.*) Right at the moment, I want never to stop seeing you. (*He sits beside her, and stares into her eyes.*) Is it possible— that I can—never stop seeing you?

GILLIAN. You can see me all you want.

SHEP. It hasn't hit you as it has me.

GILLIAN. I want you just as much as you want me.

SHEP. You do?

GILLIAN. And I'm happy. Very happy.

SHEP. (*Rises, takes his drink and crosses down below coffee table to* L. *of sofa.*) Look, Gill,—I haven't asked you, but—I guess you're free and unattached. (*He crosses up to bedroom door, then down to sofa.*)

GILLIAN. Yes.

SHEP. Well, that makes a difference—for you. You don't have to ask yourself questions. I do. I'm not free. The thing I've got to decide is —am I going to cut free?

GILLIAN. Do you want to?

SHEP. I've told you I want to. But—(*Leans over arm of sofa.*) what future is there in it?

GILLIAN. It can go on like this.

SHEP. For always?

GILLIAN. Does anything go on for always?

SHEP. One likes to think that some things can. (*Crossing up—back of sofa table to console—pours drink.*) I don't know whether this is one of those things that burn themselves out—but if it is, well, it's a hell of a fire, I know that. Maybe that's the kind that burns out quickest. I don't know. (*He crosses back to her.*) I know it's crazy to talk about love—yet—but I just wish I could be sure.

GILLIAN. Of what?

SHEP. Whether this is it. (*He puts drink on coffee table, sits next to her.*) If it's not, it's a pretty good facsimile.

GILLIAN. I think—that for me, too.

SHEP. And that will do for the answer. And now I think I'll have to use your telephone.

GILLIAN. Go right ahead.

SHEP. And this time—do you mind?—I'd like to be left alone.

GILLIAN. Of course. (*She rises, and starts for bedroom.* HE *stops her.*)

SHEP. You're amazing, do you know it? (*He kisses her passionately, and holds her.*) More than amazing!

GILLIAN. (*In his arms.*) Shep—it has hit me—quite hard. (THEY *stay together a long moment, then she leaves and goes into bedroom, closing door.* SHEP *stands where he is for a moment, then he finishes his drink in one big swallow to nerve himself—goes to phone, and then dials. He stops dialling—crosses down to* R. *of sofa—thinks of the impending call, then crosses up to phone again, dials and waits.*)

SHEP. (*Into phone.*) Is that Miss Carlson's apartment? I'd like to speak to Miss Kittredge, please. And—is there some place where she can sit down for a minute? I mean, where she can talk without being disturbed? Yes, I wish you would. (*He holds on, carrying phone to coffee table, where he nervously and absent-mindedly lights two cigarettes, one after the other. Then he answers, again, in a high, nervous voice.*) Merle? This is me. I'm—out some place. I know. That's what I'm calling about. I can't get there. I can't get there. I can't get there! No, not at all. Never. I've suddenly realized —it's no good. It's no use. Us. I mean—us! Yes, I'm afraid that is— just what I mean. I can't explain. I don't understand it, myself. Yes —yes—okay, let's have it. (*He listens, wretchedly.*) Yes . . . yes . . . Ouch! No, it's all right. I'm still here. Go on, I deserve it. Say it all. Yes, I am. Yes, I'm that. Yes, I guess I'm that, too! No, wait a minute, I'm not that! (*She has hung up. He clicks receiver hook, then slowly hangs up.*) I guess I am. (*He replaces phone, crosses to*

24

R. *chair, then calls, off.*) You can come back *now.* (GILLIAN *returns.*)
GILLIAN. (*At* R. *of stove.*) Well?
SHEP. (*Stepping to down* R. *of ottoman.*) It's done. Do you want to know about it?
GILLIAN. Do you want to tell me?
SHEP. I'd rather not.
GILLIAN. Then you needn't.
SHEP. (*Sincerely.*) Thank you.
GILLIAN. Are you unhappy about it?
SHEP. No. I ought to be—I guess. But I'm not. At all. (*Then, dismissing it all.*) Do you know something?
GILLIAN. What?
SHEP. We haven't eaten.
GILLIAN. No.
SHEP. (*Crossing to below coffee table.*) Let's go out and have caviar and champagne. How does that sound?
GILLIAN. (*She crosses to him.*) It sounds just right! (THEY *kiss, lightly.*)
SHEP. (*Takes her hand.* THEY *sit on coffee table.*) It's so ridiculous that I know nothing about you. Nothing at all.
GILLIAN. What do you want to know?
SHEP. Nothing at the moment, except about *us.* Tell me, when did you first know—that you liked me?
GILLIAN. The moment I saw you. Coming down the stairs, three days ago. I thought: "That's for me."
SHEP. Oh, you did, did you? And did nothing about it?
GILLIAN. (*Smiling.*) What can a nice girl do?
SHEP. You could have asked me down for a cocktail.
GILLIAN. I offered you a cocktail earlier this afternoon. Three times, actually. You wouldn't have it.
SHEP. Isn't that extraordinary? I never even noticed you. That sounds awful.
GILLIAN. (*Amused.*) I'm not hurt.
SHEP. Was that why you offered to arrange for me to meet Redlitch? As a come-on?
GILLIAN. I guess—in a way.
SHEP. Well, now you don't need to. Though I'd still like to meet him.
GILLIAN. You'll meet him.
SHEP. Oh, you've done something about it already?
GILLIAN. I've—set things in motion.
SHEP. When are you meeting him?

GILLIAN. Soon. (*Buzzer sounds.*)

SHEP. Damn. Don't answer that.

GILLIAN. (*Oddly.*) Do you mind if I do? (*She rises, crosses up towards door.*)

SHEP. No, I don't mind, but why?

GILLIAN. Oh—just an idea. We're going out, anyway. (*She answers buzzer. Into buzzer mouthpiece.*) Hello?

REDLITCH's VOICE. (*Off.*) Miss Holroyd?

GILLIAN. (*As before.*) Yes, who is it?

REDLITCH's VOICE. (*As before.*) This is Sidney Redlitch. You don't know me, but . . .

GILLIAN. (*Assuming astonishment.*) Mr. *Redlitch?* Yes, of course—come in. (*She hangs up and buzzes.*)

SHEP. (*Astonished, he rises, crosses* L. *and up, back of sofa table to* L.C.) Well, that is the damnedest thing! You weren't expecting him, were you?

GILLIAN. Not—quite like that. (*She steps* L.) Oh, darling, close the door!

SHEP. Oh, yes! (SHEP *closes bedroom door and returns to below* L. *pillar.* SHE *opens door.* REDLITCH *comes in. He is a man in the fifties—shambling, messy and slightly drunk.*)

GILLIAN. How do you do, Mr. Redlitch? (*She closes door.*)

REDLITCH. (*Stepping down to* R. *of* GILLIAN.) Do you know me?

GILLIAN. I've seen your picture on your book. Come in, won't you? This is Mr. Henderson. Mr. Shepherd Henderson.

REDLITCH. Oh—you've been writing to me.

SHEP. (*Smiling, crossing to him,* THEY *shake hands.* GILLIAN *steps* L.) And you've not been answering. How do you do?

REDLITCH. I've been out of town for a couple of weeks. Only got in on the train an hour ago. (*He takes off his coat, puts it and his hat on* R. *bench and comes down to* R. *of* SHEP *and* GILLIAN. *Then to* GILLIAN.) Look, I know Christmas Eve is hardly the right time for a call, but I was sitting in a bar right around the corner just now, going through my wallet, and I came across your address.

GILLIAN. (*Down* L. *of* SHEP.) Who gave you my address?

REDLITCH. Some people in Mexico. I wrote down there about a mask I'd seen, and they wrote back that you'd bought it. A kind of long black mask, with gold eyes. I wondered if you'd let me photograph it for an article I'm doing. (SHEP *offers him a cigarette.*)

GILLIAN. It's coming in the trunk I sent by rail.

REDLITCH. You don't happen to know what that mask is, do you?

26

GILLIAN. (*Playing innocent.*) No, what? (SHEP *gives* REDLITCH *a light.*)

REDLITCH. (*Heavily.*) Just one of the most potent witch-masks that I ran across down there.

GILLIAN. (*Crossing to sofa. Sits.*) Oh, they told me that, but . . .

REDLITCH. But you didn't believe it? No, nobody does. (*He turns and sees drinks on console.*) Say, you wouldn't feel like offering a poor author a glass of Christmas cheer, would you?

SHEP. (*He turns, looks at* GILLIAN *who nods and turns back to* RED-LITCH.) Yes, of course. Scotch or Bourbon?

REDLITCH. It doesn't make a bit of difference.

SHEP. Water or soda?

REDLITCH. (*Crossing to him.*) Either one. As a matter of fact, straight. With a water chaser.

SHEP. (*Crossing to console.*) Oh! I see. . . . Gillian? (REDLITCH *crosses to up* R. *of sofa.*)

GILLIAN. No, thank you. (*The door opens, and* NICKY *enters.*)

NICKY. Oh . . . Excuse me . . . I didn't know . . . (*He closes door, then sees* SHEP *and steps* R.) Oh, you're still here.

SHEP. (*With some concealed embarrassment.*) Er . . . Yes.

GILLIAN. (*Rises.*) Nicky, this is Mr. Redlitch. Mr. Sidney Redlitch. My brother. (THE MEN *shake hands. Then* NICKY *crosses to* GILLIAN, *and* REDLITCH *goes to console.*)

NICKY. Well, what do you know?

GILLIAN. Pretty good, eh? (*She crosses down to stove.*)

NICKY. I'll say. (*He crosses up to* L. *bench and puts his coat on it, then crosses to* L. *of tree.*)

REDLITCH. (*Taking his drink from* SHEP, *crosses to* L. *of ottoman.*) Thanks. Well, merry Christmas. (*He drinks.*)

GILLIAN AND SHEP. Merry Christmas!

SHEP. (*Pouring a drink for himself.*) Are you writing anything more about witchcraft, Mr. Redlitch?

REDLITCH. (*Crosses to sofa. Sits.*) Just getting ready to.

SHEP. Oh, that interests me. Very much.

REDLITCH. (*Looks at him.*) Oh? I just got my room in Brooklyn back.

GILLIAN. Brooklyn?

REDLITCH. That's where I write best. (*He flicks his ashes in his trouser cuff.*) And boy, is this one going to knock them over.

GILLIAN. (*Stepping* R.) More witchcraft, hm-m? Where this time?

REDLITCH. Right here.

GILLIAN. Here?

REDLITCH. In New York. *Witchcraft Around Us.* What do you think of that for a title? (NICKY *crosses to console, pours drink.*)

SHEP. (*Crossing to* R. *of sofa.*) It sounds provocative. What does it mean—exactly?

REDLITCH. It means exactly what it says. Witchcraft around us. All around us.

NICKY. (*Fascinated and amused, crosses to* R. *of ottoman.*) Is it?

REDLITCH. It sure is, boy. You probably thought that sort of thing was confined to the tropics and the jungles—if you thought of it at all. So did I, until now.

GILLIAN. Oh?

REDLITCH. You won't believe this, but right here—all around you—there's a whole community devoted to just that.

SHEP. That's a novel idea. (*Looks at* NICKY. THEY *laugh.*)

REDLITCH. Hell, it's not an idea. It's true.

GILLIAN. (*Leans on* L. *arm of sofa.*) How do you know?

NICKY. Tell us. (*He and* GILLIAN *sit simultaneously. From here on, he and* GILLIAN *play to each other. He, mischievously amused; she slightly so, but also very much on the alert and watchful.*)

REDLITCH. (*As* SHEP *crosses back of sofa table* L., *and sits on the* L. *sofa arm.*) Well, I've met a couple. Met them through my book. They let me in on a few things. Then, from there—well, I've made it my business to find out. You've no idea. They have their regular hangouts—cafés, bars, restaurants. Ever hear of a night club called the Zodiac?

NICKY. Yes.

SHEP. (*To* GILLIAN.) Say, isn't that the place you were talking about? That drawing . . . (*He points to it.*)

REDLITCH. What drawing? (*He crosses to it, as* NICKY *backs to* R. *of ottoman.*) Sure. She used to dance there. Who did that?

SHEP. He did. (*Points to* NICKY.)

REDLITCH. (*Up* R. *of sofa.*) And I suppose it never occurred to you that she was one?

NICKY. (*Acting incredulity.*) No!

REDLITCH. Sure. Ever look at the proprietor there?

NICKY. Don't tell me he's a witch, too!

REDLITCH. Well, when it's a man, they're called warlocks. (*He gives* SHEP *a sudden, odd, suspicious look and then turns away.*) Say, I'd like to have this for an illustration, too. (*He crosses back to below sofa.*)

NICKY. I daresay Gill would loan it to you. Go on. This is fascinating.

REDLITCH. (*Sits on sofa,* NICKY *sits on ottoman.*) Maybe you don't take it seriously . . .

GILLIAN AND NICKY. Oh, but we do!

NICKY. Tell us more about them, and their—doings.

REDLITCH. Well, then there are the places where they hold their meetings. You think of witches meeting on a blasted heath (*Looking at* SHEP.), don't you?

SHEP. (*Dryly.*) I don't think I think of their meeting at all.

GILLIAN. Where do they meet? Do you know?

REDLITCH. Sure, I know. One of their main places is up in Harlem. It's an old vaudeville house. There's another down in the Village. And sometimes they have them in a suite of offices on the top of the Woolworth Building. (*He finishes his drink, and hands the glass to* NICKY *to replenish, drinks some water and spills it over himself. He hands glass to* NICKY *who puts his own drink on coffee table, takes glass, crosses up to console and fixes another drink.*) You'd be amazed what's going on under your nose that you'd never suspect. Talk about spy-rings and organized vice—they're nothing compared to it.

SHEP. What do they look like? The witches, I mean? (NICKY *crosses back to sofa.*)

REDLITCH. Like anyone else. Like you—or you—or you. (*He points to each in turn.*) You couldn't tell them, but I could.

NICKY. (*Giving him the drinks.*) You mean you can—recognize them?

REDLITCH. Like a shot.

GILLIAN. How?

REDLITCH. (*Puts drinks on table.*) Well, that's hard to say. It's a something. A look. A feeling. I don't know. But if one were to walk in here right now, I'd know. (*He looks at* SHEP's *hand, on back of couch.* SHEP, *nervously, removes it and rises, very uncomfortably.*)

NICKY. (*Takes his glass, sits on ottoman.*) Gill, I wonder if we know any.

GILLIAN. I wonder.

REDLITCH. I'll bet you do. I bet that I could tell you names that . . .

NICKY. Oh, do!

REDLITCH. (*Leans back on sofa.*) Uh-huh. Can't do that. I'm careful. That's why there can't be any names in my book. Though I've got protection, up to a point.

SHEP. (*At stove.*) Protection?

REDLITCH. There's a woman—pretty high up in the movement. She's considered about the best there is. Well, I've got her on my side.

GILLIAN. (*With a touch of professional jealousy.*) Who's that?

REDLITCH. A Mrs. de . . . Well, I shouldn't give her name, though she's pretty open about it. Kind of flaunts it. Some of them do, you know. Go about dressed up so that people will recognize them. You may have seen this woman. She goes to opening nights in robes with Cabalistic what-d'-you-call-thems all over them.

GILLIAN. A Mrs. de Pass.

REDLITCH. That's the one. Matter of fact, I'm going up to her house a bit later.

GILLIAN. (*Alarmed.*) Tonight?

REDLITCH. Yes. She's got a party. I'll tell you another couple of things about them. Witches don't cry. Shed tears, I mean. Or blush.

SHEP. Oh, really?

REDLITCH. And if you throw them in the water, they float.

SHEP. Anyone tried that lately?

REDLITCH. (*To* GILLIAN.) And they almost all have pets. They're called "familiars." You know—familiar spirits who have to carry out their masters' bidding.

GILLIAN. (*Rising suddenly, crosses to* SHEP.) Shep, we ought to go. (NICKY *and* REDLITCH *rise.*)

REDLITCH. Oh, everyone is bored, all of a sudden.

GILLIAN. No, no, I'm not. I'm sure there is a lot of it around.

SHEP. (*Involuntarily.*) Like influenza. (GILLIAN *crosses back of sofa table, to window seat, picks up jacket.*)

REDLITCH. Okay. Okay. Make fun of it. I'm used to that. (NICKY *crosses to console, puts his drink down.*)

SHEP. (*Crosses to* REDLITCH.) No, I'm sorry, I didn't mean to. I really am interested. In fact, I'd like to hear more about it. I understand your contract with Seldens is just about up. (GILLIAN *crosses to* R. *table.*)

REDLITCH. It is.

SHEP. Well, I wish you'd lunch with me and my partner one day.

REDLITCH. (*He crosses* C.) Sure. Glad to. (*To* GILLIAN.) And if you'd let me know when that mask turns up . . . I'll give you my address. (*He gets out pencil and paper, crosses up to sofa table.*)

SHEP. Give it to me, too, will you? (*He crosses up to* REDLITCH.)

GILLIAN. (*To* NICKY, *in an undertone.*) Nicky, you know where Aunt Queenie was going tonight . . .

NICKY. (*Crossing to her.*) No. Where? Oh, yes . . .

GILLIAN. (*With an inclination of her head toward* REDLITCH *and* SHEP.) I don't think that's a good idea.

NICKY. (*With an understanding glance and nod.*) What do you want me to do?

GILLIAN. Stop it. Can you?

NICKY. Sure! (*He crosses up to console, then down to window seat, getting his records.*)

REDLITCH. (*Crosses* C., SHEP *crosses to* R. *of sofa.*) Here you are, Miss Holroyd.

GILLIAN. (*Crosses above ottoman to him, shakes hands.*) Thank you very much. I'm sorry to have to turn you out, but . . . (*Crossing to* L. *of* SHEP.)

SHEP. We do have to go out. Well, I'll call you.

NICKY. (*Crossing to* REDLITCH.) You know, I'd like to hear some more about this book. I'll walk along with you. (*He gets his coat, puts it on.*)

REDLITCH. (*Getting his coat.*) We'll stop in for a drink some place.

NICKY. Fine.

REDLITCH. (*Crossing down to* L. *of ottoman.*) Well, good-bye then.

SHEP. (*Steps* R.) I'll be in touch with you.

REDLITCH. Okay! (*As he and* NICKY *go out.*) There's a place on Third Avenue called "The Cloven Hoof" I'd like to show you. (THEY *are gone.* GILLIAN *crosses below coffee table,* L.)

SHEP. This has been the most extraordinary evening! He seemed to think that *I* was one of them! (*He comes to* GILLIAN.) And now, if we're going to have our first meal together . . .

GILLIAN. I'll get my wrap. (*She goes into bedroom.* SHEP *crosses to window seat, puts on his coat and his muffler. Then he sees carton full of presents. He picks up a couple and stands turning them over in his hands.* GILLIAN *returns, with an evening cloak, and throws it on sofa. Crossing to* L. *of sofa.*) What are you going to do with all those presents?

SHEP. Have them sent around, in the morning, I guess. With apologies. *Most* of them. (*He crosses below* R. *table.*) All these presents— and none for you.

GILLIAN. (*Crossing to below* R. *end of coffee table.*) Give me one.

SHEP. Which?

GILLIAN. Any one. Shut your eyes, and—dip. Go on. (HE *goes to window seat, closes his eyes and rootles in carton. Finally brings out a small package. He opens his eyes and looks at it.*)

SHEP. How extraordinary!

GILLIAN. (*Crossing to down* R. *of ottoman.*) Why—what is it? (HE *hands it to her, without a word.*) What is it?

SHEP. Open it. It's a locket. Rather a revolting locket, really. I was giving it to someone—it has some significance, or other.

GILLIAN. (*Stopping her unwrapping.*) Do you still want to give it to them?

SHEP. No. (SHE *unwraps package. Inside is a small jeweler's box. She opens it and takes out an old-fashioned locket.*)

GILLIAN. It's beautiful. (*She holds it up.*)

SHEP. (*Taking box and paper and putting it on* R. *table.*) You think so, too? It belonged to my—damn it, why can't one say "my mother" without sounding sentimental? (*As* SHE *starts to open it.*) You can guess what's inside.

GILLIAN. You?

SHEP. (*Nodding.*) Aged . . . (*He holds his hand at eight-year-old height.*)

GILLIAN. (*Looking at it.*) I should have met you earlier.

SHEP. (*Half amused.*) You think so?

GILLIAN. Yes, I do.

SHEP. Shall I put it on for you?

GILLIAN. If you're really sure?

SHEP. I am. (SHE *turns and* HE *fastens it around her neck.*)

GILLIAN. (*With a little satisfied smile.*) Well, then—thank you. *Very* much. (*She turns to him.*)

SHEP. (*Taking her in his arms.*) Merry Christmas, my darling.

GILLIAN. Merry Christmas to you. (THEY *kiss.*) Shall we go?

SHEP. Sure. (*He crosses to window seat, puts on his muffler—gets his hat and then turns off console lamp.* GILLIAN *gets her wrap, goes* C., *puts it on and then crosses to sofa table lamp and turns it off. She goes to door and opens it. The only light now comes from the hall outside, and from the glow of the fire, silhouetting them as they stand in the doorway.* SHEP *stands, looking back at the room.* GILLIAN *joins him.*)

GILLIAN. What are you looking at?

SHEP. This place. The place you happened to me in. This room.

GILLIAN. It's just an ordinary room.

SHEP. Not by a long shot. It may look like one, but . . . (*He shakes his head.*)

GILLIAN. Well, you'll see it again.

SHEP. (*Forcibly.*) You bet I will. (*He puts his arm around her. They turn and go out.*)

CURTAIN

32

ACT II

The same. Two weeks later. Afternoon. The stage is empty when the curtain rises. The light outside the windows is fading to darkness. The Christmas tree has gone. The Mexican mask is hanging prominently on the back wall, L. of kitchen entrance.

The door opens and GILLIAN *and* SHEP *come in.* GILLIAN *switches on the hall light.* SHEP *takes latchkey from door and puts it in his pocket.* GILLIAN *carries a large box of candy and some letters. She comes to sofa table, switches on lamp, and puts candy box down.* SHEP *takes off his coat and hat and puts them on hall bench.* GILLIAN *crosses down* L., *looking at letters.*

SHEP. (*Standing below coffee table.*) Darling, come here.

GILLIAN. (*She comes to him.*) Yes? (*He takes her in his arms and kisses her.*)

SHEP. I've been aching to do that for the last three hours. Since before lunch.

GILLIAN. Is that why you wouldn't take me to tea?

SHEP. My, but your nose stays cold a long time.

GILLIAN. I'm cold-blooded.

SHEP. (*Holds her away from him.*) I'd hardly say that. You know something? You get better all the time.

GILLIAN. Hmm-m?

SHEP. To be with. To do things with. Everything. I've never known what to do with Saturday afternoons in New York before, except wait for them to become Saturday night. This one's been wonderful. (*He crosses up* R. *to console. Puts on lamp, and crosses to window.*)

GILLIAN. (*Crossing to* L. *of sofa table, taking off her hat and gloves.*) Lunching at the Plaza—going to an art exhibit—walking down Park Avenue? The most ordinary things!

SHEP. (*Drawing drapes.*) And what a bit of magic can do to them!

GILLIAN. Magic?

SHEP. (*Crossing to window down* R.) Well, isn't it? Two weeks ago tonight we met. And they've been magic weeks. (*Draws lower drape and crosses toward* GILLIAN.)

GILLIAN. (*Starts to take off coat.*) I know. They have. They've been exactly that. Enchantment! (SHEP *starts toward her. She holds out her hand to stop him. He stops.*) No, Shep! We're going to have tea.

SHEP. (*Agreeing.*) First? . . . Right. (*He starts to kitchen, stops up R. to pick up something.*)

GILLIAN. (*Crossing to him.*) Oh, Shep, not another pin! You, who won't even pick up a newspaper!

SHEP. I've always picked up pins. Okay. I know. Sheer superstition. Doesn't mean a thing. (*Puts pin in lapel of his jacket.*)

GILLIAN. How many have you got in there already? (*She looks at his lapel.*) Four!

SHEP. I have not! (*He takes them out.*) I'll throw them in the fire.

GILLIAN. (*Quickly and unguardedly.*) No!

SHEP. Why not?

GILLIAN. It's bad luck. Yes, I'm superstitious, too. Give them to me. I'll take them. (*She takes pins from him.*)

SHEP. What are you going to do with them?

GILLIAN. (*Crossing L. to bedroom door.*) Keep them. (*Vaguely.*) They come in handy!

SHEP. What for?

GILLIAN. (*As before.*) Different things. (*She goes into bedroom, carrying her hat and coat.* SHEP *starts for kitchen again, then stops below door and looks at mask.* GILLIAN *returns, crosses down to coal box.*)

SHEP. (*Teasingly.*) Consistent, aren't you? Superstitious—yet you'll have this thing in the place, after what Redlitch said about it?

GILLIAN. (*Smiling.*) I think it's kind of friendly.

SHEP. (*Looking at its ugliness, dubiously.*) Well, not toward *me*, I don't think! (*He looks at it, then says to it, sharply and suddenly*) Boo! (*He goes into kitchen. Phone rings.* GILLIAN *answers it.*)

GILLIAN. Hello? Oh, Nicky. Well, *I've* been busy, too. Quite busy. No, not the way you think. Just busy. What can I do for you? Shep? You mean, Shepherd Henderson? Yes, I see him—now and then. What do you want with him? Well, call him. Why ask me? Well, certainly not today. I just don't want you to. Maybe I can arrange for you to meet him next week. (SHEP *returns with tea-tray, minus teapot. He puts it on coffee table, and sits, listening puzzledly.*) I can't talk now. No, I can't do that now, either. All right, then, say it over to me, and I'll correct you. Yes. Yes. No, the other way around. That's it, and count ten between the last two. Okay. What? Oh, Natalie's party? No, I'd love to, but I can't, tonight.

SHEP. Look, if this is something . . .

GILLIAN. (*Quieting him.*) Ssh! (*Back into phone.*) No, nothing's going on. No, no, don't come over. Hello, hello . . . (NICKY *has hung up.* SHE *bangs hook a couple of times, then hangs up, crosses to R. of sofa table.*)

34

SHEP. What was all that about?

GILLIAN. (*Unwrapping candy box.*) Oh, just someone I've known for ages—and ages.

SHEP. Were they asking you to coach them in a part or something?

GILLIAN. (*Puts paper in waste-basket, crosses back of R. table, and selects a candy.*) Yes—or something. But it's not important.

SHEP. Look, sweet, we've spent all our time together, all our meals and everything. It's just occurred to me, there must be people you're neglecting.

GILLIAN. No one I care about.

SHEP. I've been neglecting *everything*. There's a whole stack of manuscripts piled up by my bed—only I never seem to get there any more! Darling, why don't you go to your party tonight? (*Crossing to her.*) Maybe I'll join you there later.

GILLIAN. (*Too quickly.*) Oh, no!

SHEP. Why not?

GILLIAN. (*Evasively.*) You'd hate it.

SHEP. Do you know I haven't met a single friend of yours?

GILLIAN. And you're not going to. They're awful.

SHEP. (*He laughs.*) What are they like?

GILLIAN. (*Surprised.*) Like? They're—(*Reflecting.*) irresponsible— and malicious—and unprincipled—and *fun!*

SHEP. Well, that's something.

GILLIAN. (*Crossing to down L. of coffee table.*) I'm not sure that's not the worst part.

SHEP. (*Turns, steps L.*) Hey, what's eating you all of a sudden?

GILLIAN. (*Disturbed and restless, crosses to stove.*) I don't know. I just don't like myself very much, that's all.

SHEP. I'm crazy about you. (*Crosses above ottoman to c.*) Gillian, when are we going to get married? (SHE *turns and stares at him in astonishment.*) What's the matter?

GILLIAN. (*Stepping to sofa.*) I must have missed a chapter somewhere.

SHEP. (*At R. of sofa.*) Darling, after the last two weeks, you can't say, "This is so sudden."

GILLIAN. No, but I hadn't thought of marriage.

SHEP. (*Lightly.*) Darling, that's the *man's* remark—usually.

GILLIAN. (*Smiling, but half-serious.*) You mean you've been thinking of it—all along?

SHEP. (*Crossing below sofa, takes her hand and seats her next to him on sofa.*) Well, not all along, but—now it's getting pretty bad.

I never knew a man could feel this way. I'm going crazy. I've let everything slide. My business is shot to hell. My secretary glares at me and my partner isn't speaking to me. I can't stay in the office for wanting to get to this place, and to you. When I get here, I can't wait to get close to you. And then I never can get close enough.

GILLIAN. (*Keeping up banter.*) And how do you think marriage would cure that?

SHEP. I don't know. I don't care. But we can't go on like this.

GILLIAN. (*Leaning away.*) Darling—that's the girl's remark—usually!

SHEP. You know I'm in love with you. Marriage is the logical next step. Doesn't it seem that way to you? (SHE *does not answer.*) Gill, why are you ducking this? Tell me, be serious.

GILLIAN. (*Moving away to below coffee table.*) I don't think I'm cut out for marriage, that's all.

SHEP. In what way?

GILLIAN. (*Crossing to up R. of ottoman.*) The way I've lived . . .

SHEP. (*Rises.*) How have you lived?

GILLIAN. Selfishly—restlessly—one thing after another. (*Quickly.*) I don't mean *affairs.*

SHEP. (*Amused and relieved.*) I'm glad about that. What do you mean?

GILLIAN. (*Vaguely.*) Just—one thing after another.

SHEP. (*Crossing to her, turns her to him.*) Well, anyhow, there's a time to stop. There's a moment when we get the chance to go one of two ways for ever. But you've got to recognize the moment when it comes. This is it—for *me.* I thought for *you,* too. (*Pause.*) No?

GILLIAN. (*Slowly, very torn by an inner conflict.*) I don't know. It would mean—giving up a whole way of living—and thinking. I've wondered sometimes if I could. And wished I could.

SHEP. Settle down, you mean.

GILLIAN. You can call it that. But that's not what's worrying me.

SHEP. What is?

GILLIAN. I told you. Me.

SHEP. So long as it's not me.

GILLIAN. It's not.

SHEP. Then let me do the worrying. (*He puts his arms around her.* SHE *does not answer.*) Well?

GILLIAN. (*Slowly.*) You're tempting me.

SHEP. (*Still holding her.*) That's better.

GILLIAN. (*Stalling.*) That kettle must be boiling by now.

SHEP. (*With double meaning. He moves back.*) They don't boil if you watch them—eh? (*He goes into kitchen.* GILLIAN *stands alone.*)
GILLIAN. (*To herself.*) I wonder. I wonder if I could. Suppose he found out, afterwards. That would be bad. (*With a little giggle.*) And what would all the others say? (*She seems to hear a chuckle from the mask, and crosses up to it.*) Don't look at me like that. (*She crosses to* C., *and turns again to mask.*) I will, if I want to. (SHEP *returns, carrying teapot. He crosses with it to coffee table.* GILLIAN *keeps her eyes on him, as though measuring her whole future with him. Then she comes to sofa, sits and pours tea.* SHEP *sits* L. *of her. The silence between them is long and tense.* SHE *hands him his tea.* HE *takes cup, and they* BOTH *sip in unison. Then, with her cup still in her hand, she speaks at last.*) Shep, I will.
SHEP. (*He puts his cup on tray.*) I'd like to hear that again.
GILLIAN. I will. I want to.
SHEP. (*Moving to embrace her.*) I think you will have to put that cup down. (*He takes it from her, puts it on tray.*) Oh, darling . . . darling . . . (*He embraces her.*) Darling! (*Then, with an intake of breath.*) What do we say next? (THEY *lean back.*) Where shall we live? Shall I buy this place from you? Then we can throw the other tenants out and unconvert it? Hmm?
GILLIAN. I've only got a lease on this house. And anyway, I'd like to start somewhere afresh.
SHEP. What—again? You know, I wish you'd make a list of your past activities. A primitive art gallery on Twelfth Street. Book shop —herb shop. I can't keep up with them.
GILLIAN. (*Disturbed, she sits up.*) Shep—don't ask me questions about my past.
SHEP. (*A shade worried, but trying to laugh it off.*) You do make it sound lurid.
GILLIAN. I don't mean it that way. Though there have been—episodes. Do you want to know about them?
SHEP. (*Humorously uncomfortable.*) Er—no. I don't think I do.
GILLIAN. Well, that's the way I feel about it all. My life's been sort of—raffish—at least, seen through your eyes. And I don't want to talk about it.
SHEP. Yes, but your childhood, everything that makes you what you are—I'm jealous of these things. Oh, I know you don't feel that way. You're not jealous, in the remotest degree, about anything. You knew there was another woman—right up to the moment we met —yet you've never asked me one thing about her. Who she was,

or anything. That seems incredible to me.

GILLIAN. (*Rises, crosses to above ottoman.*) Yes, but that—whatever it was—is over. I know it is.

SHEP. Even so, just a little twinge of jealousy would be flattering.

GILLIAN. (*With a change.*) Oh, don't think I can't be jealous. I can—in my own way. It's my worst thing. Almost. That, and trying to get something for nothing. Eating my cake, and having it, too. But I'll be different from now on. I promise you, I swear!

SHEP. I don't want you different.

GILLIAN. (*Crossing L., she sits on R. arm of sofa.*) But I want to be different. Quite different.

SHEP. (*Pulling her down on sofa.*) I won't stand for it! (*He kisses her.*) I wonder if two people have ever had a romance like this before.

GILLIAN. Very few! Very few!

SHEP. Damn few.

GILLIAN. Yes. Damn few. (*Buzzer sounds.*)

SHEP. Hell! There's life breaking in.

GILLIAN. Tell it to go away.

SHEP. We've got to start meeting it again, some time. And now we've got the rest of our lives together. . . .

GILLIAN. All right. I'll be polite to it. (*She rises to go to buzzer.*)

SHEP. Maybe it's Aunt Queenie. Does she know about us, by the way?

GILLIAN. (*Coming back to sofa.*) Certainly. She's been tickled to death about it.

SHEP. Oh, not only eccentric, but immoral, too!

GILLIAN. No. Just romantic. (*She answers buzzer.*) Hello.

NICKY'S VOICE. Gill? It's Nicky.

GILLIAN. Oh, Nicky—please!

NICKY'S VOICE. I want to come up. (GILLIAN *buzzes for him. Then she turns to* SHEP.)

GILLIAN. There you are. Interruptions. (*She steps to below and R. of door.*)

SHEP. (*Crossing to up L. of door.*) We won't let him stay long. We'll get rid of him. (NICKY *enters, and sees* SHEP. *Closes door.*)

NICKY. (*Eagerly shaking hands.*) Hello! Well, how very nice. (*He turns.*) Thanks, Gill. (*He sees mask.*) Say, that's new, isn't it? Is that the one Redlitch was talking about? It looks just like the German governess we used to have. (*He takes off his coat, puts it on L. bench.* GILLIAN *goes to back of R. chair.*)

SHEP. You're quite a stranger.

NICKY. (*Stepping down* C.) That's right. Not since Christmas Eve.

SHEP. Where have you been?

NICKY. Believe it or not, in Brooklyn!

GILLIAN. What for?

NICKY. I've got a hotel room there. It's handier for work.

GILLIAN. Work? *You?*

NICKY. Yes, dear. And it's not nearly as tough as standing in line for unemployment insurance.

GILLIAN. (*Going to him.*) Nicky. What are you up to?

NICKY. I've got a surprise for you. (*To* SHEP.) For you, too. (*Holding up envelope.*) Sid's new book. Sid Redlitch.

SHEP. (*Taking envelope.*) What, already?

NICKY. Oh, not all of it. This is just an outline, and the first two chapters. But it will give you an idea.

SHEP. (*Sitting on* R. *of sofa, looking through its contents.*) Well, that's pretty quick.

NICKY. Oh, we've been at it, night and day.

GILLIAN. Did you say "we"?

NICKY. (*Smugly.*) Yes, dear. (*Goes to her.*) *Witchcraft Around Us,* by Sidney Redlitch and Nicholas Holroyd. With illustrations by N. Holroyd.

GILLIAN. You mean—you're writing it with him? (HE *nods, beaming.* SHE *giggles, and crosses to back of* R. *chair.* NICKY *follows her.*) Oh—oh, what fun!

SHEP. But—what do you know about that sort of thing?

NICKY. I know as much as he does. (*Airily, steps* L. *to ottoman.*) You —pick things up.

SHEP. (*Rises.*) Well, this is a surprise. Isn't it, Gill?

GILLIAN. (*With twinkling eyes.*) It certainly is.

SHEP. We've got a surprise for you, too. (*Crosses to* GILLIAN. *He puts his arm around her.*) Think you could stand me as a brother-in-law?

NICKY. (*Steps down* L. *of ottoman.*) Do you mean it?

SHEP. Well, I do. Don't you? (*He turns to* GILLIAN. *She nods.*)

NICKY. (*Lightly, almost casually.*) Well, for goodness' sake. Well, bless your hearts. (*He kisses* GILLIAN.) Congratulations, darling. (*Shakes hand with* SHEP.) Both of you.

SHEP. Thanks.

NICKY. (*Backing to* L. *of ottoman.*) That was pretty quick, too, wasn't it?

SHEP. No, not at all!

NICKY. (*With sudden realization.*) Say you've been here all along.

SHEP. Well, not all along.

GILLIAN. (*Quickly.*) Shep, I'd like to talk to Nicky. Do you mind?

SHEP. To exchange some sentimental tears?

GILLIAN. Well, maybe. (*Sits in R. chair.*)

SHEP. (*Crossing up to door.*) I'll go up to my apartment for a bit.

NICKY. (*Going to door with him.*) Why don't you look that book over now?

SHEP. Now?

NICKY. Sure. It won't take you long. It's good.

SHEP. Well, I might glance at it.

NICKY. Fine!

SHEP. Bless you, Gill dearest. (*He exits.* GILLIAN *and* NICKY *smile at each other.*)

NICKY. (*Smiles, then crossing down to R. of sofa.*) Well, well, well! Marriage, no less.

GILLIAN. Uh-huh.

NICKY. What fun!

GILLIAN. It is—very.

NICKY. (*Kneels on ottoman.*) Between the two of us, he's going to have quite a time.

GILLIAN. The two of us?

NICKY. Me and my book. I'm going to need your help. You know I've never kept up with all the manifestoes.

GILLIAN. (*Lightly.*) Oh, invent anything you like. What's it matter?

NICKY. (*Crossing down to coffee table.*) Oh, I can't. Sid's a stickler for accuracy.

GILLIAN. (*Sitting up.*) What? Nicky, you're not giving him the truth?

NICKY. Sure, I am.

GILLIAN. But I thought this book was a joke. You don't mean he knows about you?

NICKY. (*Crosses to L. of ottoman.*) Of course. You've no idea the things I've shown him and told him.

GILLIAN. (*Alarmed, she crosses to R. of ottoman.*) You didn't tell him about me?

NICKY. No, darling. I told him it was I who summoned him. But if you want to take credit . . .

GILLIAN. (*Interrupting, angrily.*) I do not want to take credit. (*Crossing to L. of* NICKY.) Oh, Nicky, why—why did you do this? Don't you know by now it never pays to tell outsiders?

NICKY. (*Blandly.*) Darling, it's going to pay beautifully. I gather

Shep has made Sid a very generous offer.

GILLIAN. You mean that's what Shep is reading upstairs now? (HE *nods.*) You can't publish that book. I wont let you.

NICKY. What harm can it do to you? There are no names in it.

GILLIAN. But your name is going to be on it, and it's too close to home to be safe. Nicky, Shep doesn't know about me. And he's not going to.

NICKY. (*Ribbing her.*) Oh, I suppose you'll tell me you're going to renounce, too.

GILLIAN. (*Crossing to below* C. *of sofa.*) I have renounced.

NICKY. (*As before.*) Since when?

GILLIAN. Well, actually, since half an hour ago.

NICKY. (*Growing serious.*) You don't mean this marriage is on the level?

GILLIAN. Uh-huh.

NICKY. That's crazy. You can't be in love with him. What are you marrying him for, anyway?

GILLIAN. Because I want to. (*Urgently.*) That's why you've got to stop that book.

NICKY. (*Firmly.*) I'm sorry, dear, but no. It's too important to me.

GILLIAN. (*Equally firmly, crosses to him.*) It's more important to me!

NICKY. (*Quietly.*) No, dear, I'm sorry. (*Crossing above ottoman to* R. *of it.*) But quite firmly—*no!*

GILLIAN. (*After a moment.*) Very well then, I'll have to do something about it.

NICKY. You don't mean "pull one"? I thought you'd retired?

GILLIAN. (*Again, after a second.*) Yes, I have. But I'll make a farewell appearance to stop this!

NICKY. We've got people on our side, remember.

GILLIAN. Mrs. de Pass? Well, I'm better than that old battle-axe.

NICKY. Yes, but she can take it up higher. To the big boys. She'll get the whole organization back of it!

GILLIAN. (*Crossing to ottoman.*) That bunch of phony fuddy-duddies! There isn't one of them that give anyone a flat tire, without having to go to bed for a week! (*She moves to him.*) Now, will you bring me every copy in existence, or am I going to have to go to work? You know I can, don't you? (*She picks up tea-tray and crosses back to* NICKY.) Think it over while I take these out. (*She goes out to the kitchen with it.* NICKY *stands baffled and angry.*)

NICKY. Mrs. de Pass—(*He goes to telephone, dials a number and gets busy signal.*) Damn! (*He hangs up, steps* R.) No, wait a minute.

(*Then he gets an idea, lifting receiver again.*) Actatus, Catipta, Marnutus . . . (GILLIAN *returns, carrying cat.*)

GILLIAN. (*Silkily.*) Nicky, I wouldn't do that, whatever it is. If I were you. Well, what's it to be? Yes or no?

NICKY. (*Crosses to* R. *of ottoman.*) Not on your life.

GILLIAN. Very well, then. (*She sits, nursing cat and stroking it.*) Pye - Pye - Pyewacket. Eloas, Bejulet, Phidibus. I don't want that book to be published. Do you hear? Not by anyone.

NICKY. (*Warningly.*) Gill, watch out.

GILLIAN. And that'll teach you to threaten me with the organization.

NICKY. Okay, you asked for it. I'm going to see that your little romance goes on the rocks, my girl. Shep's going to know all about you. And before the day is out, too. (SHEP *re-enters.* NICKY *crosses* L. *above coffee table.*)

SHEP. (*Closing door, coming down* C.) Oh, you're still here, Nicky. Good. Hello, there's Pyewacket again. I haven't seen him in a long time.

NICKY. (*Crossing up to sofa* L.) What are you going to do with Pye, now?

GILLIAN. I'm going to put him out. (*She takes cat into kitchen.*)

NICKY. I meant, now that you two are getting married.

SHEP. Oh, did she tell you that he doesn't like me? Can't bear me to touch him, for some reason? (GILLIAN *returns, comes to back of* R. *chair.*)

NICKY. (*Crossing to below sofa,* C.) Did you read it? How did you like it?

SHEP. Do you want me to talk in front of Gillian?

NICKY. Sure. Why not?

SHEP. Gill, I'm afraid Nicky here has been a bad boy. I don't think Aunt Queenie's the only member of your family who goes in for practical jokes.

NICKY. You think this book's a joke?

SHEP. It's crazy. You should call it *What Every Young Witch Ought to Know.* How you imagined for one instant that I'd fall for it! (*To* GILLIAN.) I've just been talking to Redlitch on the phone and he said that Nicky had convinced him that he was one of them. I think that was going a little far.

NICKY. (*Crossing to sofa.*) Did he tell you how he got here, in the first place?

SHEP. (*Stepping* L.) Yes, I had all that. Luminous paint, or something. And all your references, including a Mrs. de Pass, who seems to be some sort of Head Witch or something. But now the joke's over. So you'd better tell Redlitch the whole thing was a gag, or that book will have to find another publisher.

NICKY. (*After a pause, he smiles.*) No, I don't guess any other publisher would be any good, either. *Now.* Do you, Gill?

GILLIAN. (*Faintly alarmed.*) Nicky, what are you up to?

NICKY. (*Gaily. Steps* R.) Not a thing, darling. Okay, Shep, I guess it was silly of me to think you'd believe it—like that. Well, goodbye—and—no hard feelings? (*Shakes hands with* SHEP.)

SHEP. You're an ass, Nicky.

NICKY. (*Crosses up, gets his coat, and at door turns, to* GILLIAN *smiling.*) So long, Gill. You'll be hearing from me. Later in the day. (*He exits.* SHEP *crosses to* R. *of sofa.*)

SHEP. Is anything the matter?

GILLIAN. (*Crossing to* R. *of* R. *table.*) No.

SHEP. You look peculiar. Nothing wrong between you and Nicky?

GILLIAN. No.

SHEP. (*Crossing to coal box, takes shovelful.*) Really, the young scamp. I don't think he's going to have an easy time with Redlitch. (*He stoops to mend the fire. There is a long pause.* GILLIAN *raises her head, with terrific determination.*)

GILLIAN. (*Crosses to above* R. *chair.*) Shep, I've got to tell you something.

SHEP. (*Back to her.*) What?

GILLIAN. (*She makes two desperate, determined efforts, up* R. *of chair, down* R. *of chair, and then she crosses to below* R. *table, and nothing comes out. Then, at last, her voice strangling so that it comes out almost in a squeak, she turns to him, steps* L.) Shep—I'm one.

SHEP. (*Turning.*) What did you say?

GILLIAN. I said—I'm one. I was one.

SHEP. One what?

GILLIAN. One of the people that that book's about. Nicky's one, too!

SHEP. (*Rises, and with a roar of laughter.*) Oh, that's what it is. (*Puts poker back.*) He's persuaded you to come in on it. (*He sits on sofa.*) I suppose that's to carry on the joke? Sorry, dear, but it won't work.

GILLIAN. (*Crossing to above ottoman.*) No, no, no! You've got it all wrong! Shep—you've got to listen. I've got to try and explain something to you.

SHEP. Not if it's to prove to me that Nicky is a witch. No.

GILLIAN. (*Irritated, steps* L.) The word is "warlock."

SHEP. Well, we don't have to get technical about it!

GILLIAN. (*Crosses and sits next to him.*) You don't believe there are such things—at all?

SHEP. No, dear, and it's no good trying to make me.

GILLIAN. No matter who told you?

SHEP. No matter who told me.

GILLIAN. (*Turning away from him.*) I wish I could trust that!

SHEP. (*Sensing her real distress.*) Look, nobody's threatening you with anything, are they? Nicky isn't?

GILLIAN. (*Crossing down to below ottoman.*) I guess—in a way—he —is.

SHEP. Well, he can go to hell. What is it? Threatening to tell something about you, to me? (*He crosses to her.*)

GILLIAN. Yes.

SHEP. Well, that's easily dealt with.

GILLIAN. How?

SHEP. Tell me yourself.

GILLIAN. (*Loudly and angrily.*) That's what I'm trying to do!

SHEP. Well, what is it? Something in your past that you didn't want questions asked about?

GILLIAN. Yes!

SHEP. What then? What have you been up to? Have you been engaging in un-American activities?

GILLIAN. (*Crossing* R.) No. I'd say very American. (*Turns to him.*) Early American! Shep—look—(*Crossing below him to coffee table.*) you say you don't believe in anything supernatural. How about superstitions? Picking up pins?

SHEP. There's nothing in that. That's just habit.

GILLIAN. (*Stepping up.*) Yes, but what's the habit based on? Isn't it just in case there were something governing those things?

SHEP. No. Not at all.

GILLIAN. Shep, there is something. (*With a breath, steps* R.) There are the laws of gravity. . . .

SHEP. (*Amused.*) So I've always heard.

GILLIAN. I don't mean you can set those aside—exactly . . .

SHEP. That's a relief.

GILLIAN. But there are ways of—well—altering things.

SHEP. (*As before.*) Are there?

GILLIAN. Manipulating things for yourself.

SHEP. How interesting!

GILLIAN. Short cuts to getting your own way.

SHEP. (*Sitting on ottoman.*) And just what are those?

GILLIAN. (*Stepping up.*) Shep, the people who live by those short cuts are the people who—I've got to say it—use magic.

SHEP. (*Totally disbelieving.*) Magic?

GILLIAN. Shep, there is such a thing as magic. I know, I can do it.

SHEP. You can?

GILLIAN. Yes.

SHEP. Well, do it, then. Show me some.

GILLIAN. (*After a tempted pause, crosses down below coffee table.*) No!

SHEP. Oh, come on.

GILLIAN. No, I mustn't. It would go on and on. It always does. I've broken down once already this afternoon. (*She sits on R. end of table.*)

SHEP. (*Immensely tickled.*) You have? What did you do?

GILLIAN. I stopped that book being published.

SHEP. Oh, no, you didn't. That's my province. Sorry to spoil your story, but I decided I wasn't going to publish it after I'd read two pages.

GILLIAN. (*Angrily.*) I didn't say I stopped *you* publishing it. (*Crossing* L. *of table.*) I stopped *anyone* publishing it!

SHEP. (*Still amused.*) Oh, you can do that?

GILLIAN. Yes!

SHEP. Oh, very useful. What did you do?

GILLIAN. (*After a second.*) I can't tell you. It would sound too silly.

SHEP. No. Come on. What *did* you do?

GILLIAN. I put on a spell.

SHEP. And how does one "put on a spell"?

GILLIAN. I used Pyewacket.

SHEP. (*Still kidding her.*) You mean—you spoke to him about it? And what's he supposed to do? Go out and call on all the publishers? And talk them out of it? Is Pyewacket a witch too?

GILLIAN. He's a—familiar! (*She crosses up to* L. *of sofa table.*)

SHEP. (*Beginning to get angry.*) A what? Oh, yes, I remember, a pet who's supposed to do his master's bidding. Gill, what the hell are you getting at? (*He crosses to up* R. *end of sofa.*)

GILLIAN. (*Turning to him,* L. *of sofa.*) I'll tell you other things. The luminous paint—that was true. Only, it wasn't Nicky. It was I. You saw me doing it, even. You thought that it was indoor fireworks. And your coming here. You remember how that happened?

45

Your telephone went out of order.

SHEP. That was Providence.

GILLIAN. No, that was Nicky! He put it out of order.

SHEP. Well, I've heard of *repair* men! Why would Nicky do that? (*Sits on sofa.*)

GILLIAN. As a prank. That's what he uses it all for, mainly. (*Crossing R. below coffee table, to R. chair.*) Playing tricks. Turning all the lights on Fifty-seventh Street green at the same moment. That, and for his sex life.

SHEP. Look, Gill, you're going crazy. (*Crosses to C.*) I don't know about Nicky's sex life, but Redlitch coming here—my phone going out of order—even the lights on Fifty-seventh Street—damn it, those things are coincidences.

GILLIAN. (*Urgently.—Goes to him, C.*) They look like coincidences. They have to. You can't do it any other way. I can't bring Niagara Falls down to Grand Central Station, or turn the house into the Taj Mahal. It doesn't work that way. There's always a rational explanation—if you want it.

SHEP. Then I'll take the rational explanation.

GILLIAN. (*Turning away, to R. chair.*) Just as you took the rational explanation of us.

SHEP. What's that?

GILLIAN. (*Sitting, desperately.*) There—now, I've said it.

SHEP. You mean—that was . . .?

GILLIAN. Yes. That was!

SHEP. (*Steps up C.*) Now, wait a minute. . . .

GILLIAN. Why? You thought it strange enough yourself when it happened. You called the whole thing magic, only this afternoon.

SHEP. I didn't mean it literally.

GILLIAN. Well, was it rational, what happened to you here on Christmas Eve?

SHEP. It happened . . .

GILLIAN. How? Think back. What did happen? You came in here to use the telephone. It was busy. Then you got your number. (*She crosses her legs.*) Can you remember what happened next?

SHEP. I can remember every single thing. You went into the kitchen. I made my call. . . . You came back with the cat. . . .

GILLIAN. Go on.

SHEP. I went to the door—turned back—and suddenly I seemed to see you for the first time . . . And you were in my arms. . . .

GILLIAN. You've left out something. What did I do before that?

SHEP. You didn't do anything. You sat down and you talked to the cat. . . . (*He stops and stares at her, then, crossing to below sofa.*) Goddamn it! No, I won't believe it!

GILLIAN. (*Crossing to* R. *of ottoman.*) What made you suddenly take me in your arms?

SHEP. Because I wanted to. More than I've ever wanted to do anything in my whole life. (*He crosses to* L. *of ottoman.*) And you think you made me do it? Why? What for?

GILLIAN. Because I wanted you to. So I did that.

SHEP. You mean I had nothing to do with it, at all?

GILLIAN. I'm sorry, Shep. It's true. These powers do exist. All kinds of powers. All you've got to do is use them.

SHEP. You mean, everyone's got them? I could do things? (*He gestures.*)

GILLIAN. I guess you might do—some things. If someone showed you how. Don't ever let them.

SHEP. (*Crossing to* R. *chair.*) Don't worry about that!

GILLIAN. (*Crossing to up* L. *of ottoman.*) It's bad. The whole thing's bad.

SHEP. (*Turns to her.*) Why is it bad?

GILLIAN. It's habit-forming! (SHEP *laughs.*) You don't know. I do. I've lived among it. And I know what it can do to you. It's like pulling rank, or abusing influence. And it can destroy you as a person. Well, now you know, I've told you. (*She crosses to him.*) And I don't have to worry about anyone else telling you now.

SHEP. (*Embraces her.*) You don't have to worry about anything, any more.

GILLIAN. You don't believe a word of it, do you?

SHEP. I certainly do!

GILLIAN. (*Hopefully.*) You do?

SHEP. I believe you cast an absolutely wonderful spell on me, and I'm crazy about it. (*He kisses her. There is a knock on the door.*) Oh, damn . . . Don't answer it.

GILLIAN. (*Pulling reluctantly away.*) Darling, now that we've got the rest of our lives together . . .? (SHEP *goes to* R. *of sofa. She goes to door, opens it.* MISS HOLROYD *is there.*) Oh . . . Aunt Queenie!

MISS HOLROYD. (*Comes in as* GILLIAN *closes door.*) Hello, darling. Oh, hello, Shep, too! (GILLIAN *gestures to her to sit down.*) No, darling, I'm not staying, but something wonderful happened to me this afternoon, and I've simply got to tell you.

GILLIAN. (*Crossing to* SHEP.) Well, tell us, then.

MISS HOLROYD. Well, Gill, you know how utterly lost I've been here —without the use of my kitchen—or anything. Well, this afternoon, I met a lady at the Roxy—in the Ladies' Room. My pocketbook fell open, and some things dropped out—some pamphlets— and—well, we got to talking and *we* found we had a great deal in common. (*Crossing to her.*) . . . You know what I mean?

GILLIAN. (*Amused.*) I think I do.

SHEP. I don't. (*He sits on* R. *sofa arm.*)

MISS HOLROYD. Well, we had a soda together, she and I, and she told me about the club she lives in—a place where I can do anything I want. She said there was a vacancy right now, so I thought I'd let her introduce me, and then I could pay my entrance fee right away. (*Crossing to* R. *chair.*) I'm dining with Mrs. de Pass tonight, and it's right around the corner. (*At mention of Mrs. de Pass,* SHEP *rises, does a prodigious take.*) Why, what's the matter, Shep?

SHEP. (*Crossing below* GILLIAN *to* MISS HOLROYD.) Did you say Mrs. de Pass?

MISS HOLROYD. Why—do you know her?

SHEP. Gill—you don't mean that she . . . (*He indicates* MISS HOLROYD. GILLIAN *nods.*) Oh, no!!

MISS HOLROYD. What's this all about?

GILLIAN. (*Crosses to* SHEP.) Auntie, I'd better tell you. Shep—knows. I told him.

MISS HOLROYD. Oh, how wonderful. And is he—(*Hopefully.*) sympathetic?

SHEP. Now, wait a minute. Let's get this straight. You mean that she thinks she's one, too?

MISS HOLROYD. (*Proudly.*) Yes, Shep. How else do you think I got into your apartment, when the door was locked?

SHEP. (*Steps to her.*) You mean you can get through locked doors?

MISS HOLROYD. Usually.

SHEP. Could you get through that one if I locked it?

MISS HOLROYD. I think so.

SHEP. (*Steps up to door, opens it and takes out key.*) Good! Come along!

MISS HOLROYD. (*Follows him. She stops, looks at* GILLIAN, *who waves a forbidding finger.*) No. I mustn't. I can't.

SHEP. (*Closing door again.*) No. I suspected that. (*Crosses to sofa.*)

MISS HOLROYD. (*To* GILLIAN.) Well, you do it then.

GILLIAN. (*Crosses to her.*) No, Auntie. I've stopped. Shep and I are getting married.

48

MISS HOLROYD. (*Crossing to back of* R. *table.*) Oh, how lovely! How exciting! But, if he knows . . .

GILLIAN. That makes no difference. I've stopped.

MISS HOLROYD. (*Very disappointed, crosses to* L. *of chair.*) Oh, I'm sorry, Shep, about the door.

SHEP. I'm sorry, too.

MISS HOLROYD. It would have been such fun!

SHEP. Yes, I'd have liked to see it.

MISS HOLROYD. (*To* GILLIAN.) Well, darling, now you're getting married, you won't think I'm deserting you? (*The cries of a cat are heard.*) Why, what's that?

GILLIAN. That's Pyewacket. It must be his dinner time. (*She looks at her watch.*) Goodness, it's long past. I forgot all about him. Will you excuse me. (*She goes into kitchen.*)

SHEP. We shall miss you here.

MISS HOLROYD. (*Crossing to him.*) Oh, how nice of you. I don't know why I had to come and tell you. But I just felt an impulse. An irresistible impulse, to come.

SHEP. Did you? What's this place you're moving into? A sort of Witch's Hostel?

MISS HOLROYD. Yes, they have a communal kitchen we can all use for our brewing!

SHEP. Oh, for God's sake! (*Crosses* L. *and sits on sofa.*)

MISS HOLROYD. (*Crossing to* R. *of sofa.*) I know how hard it is to take in, at first, Shep. I don't know how much Gillian has told you about it all. About that spell she put on you?

SHEP. Yes, I had all that.

MISS HOLROYD. Maybe I should lend you some books, to explain things to you. They helped me a lot.

SHEP. Did they?

MISS HOLROYD. Yes. Of course, I always knew that I had something, but I thought it was artistic temperament. I don't think I would ever have become a witch, if my parents had let me go on the stage.

SHEP. You might have combined your talents. Gone into vaudeville and done card tricks.

MISS HOLROYD. Oh, I've never had any real talent, in either direction. Just itty-bitty ones. Gillian's the one who's really gifted.

SHEP. Miss Holroyd, you don't really believe that Gillian has any powers?

MISS HOLROYD. I know she has.

SHEP. Name me one thing she has ever done.

49

MISS HOLROYD. Wonderful things. Those thunderstorms. While she was in college on account of (*Intimately.*) you-know-who!

SHEP. (*Irritable.*) I have no idea who.

MISS HOLROYD. Your friend. Merle Kittredge.

SHEP. (*Crossing down* L.) Oh, nonsense! Gillian has never heard of Merle Kittredge.

MISS HOLROYD. (*Steps down stage.*) But, of course she has! I told her myself that you were getting married. That's why she went after you with Pyewacket.

SHEP. (*Stopping and staring at her.*) I beg your pardon?

MISS HOLROYD. Oh, but I promise you she wouldn't have used magic, if she'd had time for the usual feminine methods. No matter how great enemies she and Miss Kittredge were.

SHEP. (*Crossing to below* C. *of sofa.*) You mean—she went after me because of Merle?

MISS HOLROYD. Well—she thought you very attractive, already. You've no idea how much she likes you. Or, perhaps you have. . . .

SHEP. (*Steps in.*) Miss Holroyd, what are you trying to say?

MISS HOLROYD. Well, Shep—with us, it's like the Saints.

SHEP. Saints?

MISS HOLROYD. Yes, only the other way around! At least, that's what the books say. Saints love everyone. Just everyone. With no thought of themselves. But with us, it's just the contrary.

SHEP. (*Crossing down* R. *to window.*) Look, maybe I'd better read some of those books of yours, after all.

MISS HOLROYD. (*Follows him, crossing to* L. *of* R. *chair.*) Yes, Shep, then you'll see how impractical—well, impossible,—*love* is. Not sex. Sex is allowed. In fact, it's almost encouraged! (*Steps down* L. *of chair.*) But, of course, you must know that.

SHEP. (*Turning, angrily.*) Miss Holroyd . . .

MISS HOLROYD. Oh, no, Shep, can't I be Auntie now?

SHEP. Miss Holroyd, I don't think we had better go on with this.

MISS HOLROYD. (*Backs a step or two.*) Oh, dear, have I been too bold? (GILLIAN *returns from kitchen, crossing to above table.*)

GILLIAN. Pyewacket is acting very strangely. I had to coax and coax him.

MISS HOLROYD. (*Crossing up to* GILLIAN.) I must go, darling. I was late, even before I came. But I couldn't resist it. I just couldn't resist the urge to come.

GILLIAN. (*With a sudden suspicion, crosses to* MISS HOLROYD.) Auntie, Nicky didn't send you, did he?

MISS HOLROYD. (*Vaguely and innocently.*) Nicky? No. I just passed Nicky on the street. He waved to me—rather a funny kind of wave, but . . . Darling, I must trot. (GILLIAN *crosses up, opens door as* MISS HOLROYD *crosses up.*) Good-bye. Good-bye, Shep—*dear!* (*She goes out.* GILLIAN *closes door, crosses to* R. *of ottoman.*)

SHEP. (*After a moment he crosses above table to chair.*) Gillian, there are some things I want to ask you. Have you told me the truth —about yourself?

GILLIAN. (*Steps above ottoman.*) Yes.

SHEP. And about us?

GILLIAN. Yes. Why?

SHEP. You didn't tell me that you know Merle Kittredge. You did know her, didn't you? You were at college together. You knew about her and me, too, didn't you? You knew from the beginning? And that was why you went after me, deliberately, to spite her.

GILLIAN. (*Steps* R.) No, not to spite her.

SHEP. Why, then?

GILLIAN. Because I wanted you.

SHEP. Because you were in love with me?

GILLIAN. (*Crossing to down* L. *of ottoman.*) How could I be in love with you? I didn't know you.

SHEP. (*Crosses toward her.*) Are you in love with me now? (*Silence.*)

GILLIAN. (*After a moment, evasively.*) I'm more in love with you than I've ever been with anyone. . . .

SHEP. (*Crosses to her, down* C.) Can you be in love, at all? Can you?

GILLIAN. (*Crossing down to coffee table.*) I don't know. I never have, but then . . . I've never felt about anyone as I do about you, either. (*Turns to him.*) How does one *tell* if one's in love.

SHEP. One knows.

GILLIAN. But how?

SHEP. (*Slowly.*) Could you go on without me? I think that's the best test. If I wasn't there? Could you?

GILLIAN. I'd—have to, wouldn't I?

SHEP. And there's the answer. (*He turns away, up* R.C.)

GILLIAN. (*Follows him.*) But wouldn't I?

SHEP. Maybe. But you shouldn't feel that you could. Why do you think it's hitting me the way it is? To find out the whole thing was a frame-up—of whatever kind—to find that you just haven't been there, the whole time?

GILLIAN. (*Turning away, deeply unhappy.*) I don't think I knew. (*Sits on ottoman.*)

SHEP. Knew what?

GILLIAN. What I was doing. That it would be like this. I'm sorry. (*She puts her hand to her head.*)

SHEP. (*Angrily.*) That's great. And you needn't pretend to cry. Because you can't do that, either, if I remember rightly.

GILLIAN. (*Angrily.*) I'm not crying. (*Then, with realization, she rises and turns to* SHEP.) Oh, so you believe it, now.

SHEP. (*Crossing up to door.*) Of course I don't believe it—not a Goddamn word of it! (*A pause. Then he crosses down to* R. *of ottoman.*) Can you people take off spells that you put on? Because I think you'd better.

GILLIAN. (*Urgently, stepping back.*) No, no, I wouldn't do that. No, I won't! I won't!

SHEP. (*Again, after a pause.*) Okay! (*He goes to door, picking up his coat.*)

GILLIAN. Where are you going?

SHEP. I don't know, but I'm getting the hell out of here. For good and all!

GILLIAN. No, no, you can't.

SHEP. Oh, yes, I can! I don't know how one deals with witches—but watch me, you just watch me! (*Opens door.*) And don't think just because you put a spell on me, that I'm coming back. Because I'm not. Ever. (*He goes out, slamming door.*)

GILLIAN. (*Urgently, moving forward.*) Shep! (*Then she stops.*) The spell! He'll have to come back. (*Front door is heard to slam.*) Won't he? (*She starts to window. Then, suddenly, door bursts open, and* SHEP *breaks in again. He looks wild and utterly bewildered. He takes one step forward, then freezes, staring at* GILLIAN. *After a second, and as though struggling.*)

SHEP. What am I doing here? NO! No! Good God, No! (*He retreats slowly, as though fighting conflicting forces, and as though his feet were in glue.*) No! No!! No!!! (*He manages to exit and to slam door again.*)

CURTAIN

ACT III

SCENE 1

The scene is the same, later on that night. The mask, which was on the wall, is now broken into two pieces, lying on the chair and on

52

the floor. Only the console lamp is lighted.
GILLIAN *sits in window-seat, staring out into the street, lighted only by street-lamp. After a moment,* NICKY *enters, silently, and closes door. He sees broken fragments of mask, and registers them. Then he steps forward.*

NICKY. (*Gaily.*) Ah, a dull moment around here.
GILLIAN. (*Rising and turning.*) Nicky, how did you get in?
NICKY. (*Crossing up, putting his coat on* R. *bench. He turns on hall light.*) Don't ask silly questions. Through the door. Where's Shep?
GILLIAN. Out some place.
NICKY. You two haven't had a quarrel, or anything, have you?
GILLIAN. (*Coldly—crossing to* R. *table.*) No, not a quarrel. Just a visitor. Thank you, Nicky.
NICKY. (*Picking up pieces of the mask.*) Say, what's this? Goodness, someone's been careless.
GILLIAN. No one has been careless.
NICKY. (*Putting mask on sofa table and turning on lamp.*) What a pity it got broken! It would come in so handy right now. Don't tell me Shep broke this.
GILLIAN. You know perfectly well who did it.
NICKY. (*Crossing* C., *above ottoman.*) Yes, you. But was it in reform or anger? Not just because Shep walked out on you?
GILLIAN. (*Crossing to back of* R. *chair.*) Nicky, you've seen him. Where?
NICKY. At Sid's place. He came straight there from you. (GILLIAN *is already halfway to phone.* NICKY *moves* R.) Oh, it's no good your calling him. He isn't there now.
GILLIAN. Where is he?
NICKY. (*Crossing to up* R. *of ottoman.*) Well, that, I'm afraid I can't tell you.
GILLIAN. (*Comes down to* R. *of sofa.*) He's not with Merle? He's not thinking of Merle, is he?
NICKY. No, but I think he thinks he ought to be. (*Crossing to ottoman.*) After all, maybe he's still in love with her, underneath.
GILLIAN. (*Crossing to below* R. *chair.*) Don't think I haven't thought of that. I've been sitting here battling with the temptation to take the spell off. That's when I broke the mask. Oh, but if I leave things as they are, he'll still love me, and loathe me for it. (*She sits.*)
NICKY. (*Steps toward her.*) Yes, I don't think it was very smart of you to tell him all about the spell. Don't you know what it always

53

says on love potions? "Shake well, and don't tell."

GILLIAN. This is what happens to you. You think you're getting away with something, and you forfeit almost everything. You end up in a little world of separateness from everyone. That's what I've found out. (*A knock on door.* SHE *rises and backs down* R. *of table.*) Who's that? It can't be Shep. Shep's got his key. (*Knock is repeated.* NICKY *opens door.* SHEP *is outside.*) Shep!

SHEP. (*In doorway,* R. *of* NICKY.) Nicky, I want to talk to Gillian. Alone. Will you clear out? It won't take more than a couple of minutes.

NICKY. Sure. I'll just get some cigarettes around the corner. (*He takes his coat over his arm and goes, closing door.*)

GILLIAN. (*Urgently, as soon as door is closed. She steps up* R. *of table.*) Shep, won't you please . . .?

SHEP. (*Interrupting firmly.*) Listen to me. I've got something to say, and I want to say it fast. I don't want to be here. And I wouldn't be, only I was told I had to, so here I am. (*Pause.*) For your information, I have been to Mrs. de Pass.

GILLIAN. (*Appalled. She steps to above* R. *table.*) Oh, no! Why? What for?

SHEP. For a hair of the dog that bit me. After listening to Redlitch and to Nicky, they convinced me that there might be just a shred of truth in all this stuff of yours, so I thought I'd take a fling at the full treatment. I'd heard quite a lot about this de Pass dame from all of you, so I got Redlitch to take me up there.

GILLIAN. (*Aghast.*) Not to get her to take the spell off? Oh, no!

SHEP. (*Roughly.*) What the hell else?

GILLIAN. And—did she? Shep, did she?

SHEP. Sure, she did. For whatever it was worth.

GILLIAN. How?

SHEP. With a whole lot of hocus-pocus and a very dirty old parrot. From what I've seen, it's a lot more complicated to take a spell off than to put one on.

GILLIAN. (*Bitterly.*) It would be. For her. (*Pause.*) And how do you feel now?

SHEP. I don't feel anything, except Goddamned mad.

GILLIAN. At me?

SHEP. At the whole business. And at myself for getting into it. Going up, hat in hand, to a crummy joint like that . . . having to learn a little poem . . . saying, "Yes, ma'am," and "No, ma'am" to that old bag. . . . It's stomach-turning, and humiliating!

54

GILLIAN. (*Ashamed. She turns away.*) I know. Don't tell me.

SHEP. (*Ignoring her.*) To say nothing of being out a hell of a lot of dough, into the bargain.

GILLIAN. (*Turns to him.*) Why, what did she charge you?

SHEP. Plenty.

GILLIAN. How much?

SHEP. I don't want to go into it. Any of it. The only reason that I came was that she said the thing wouldn't be complete until I'd seen you and told you.

GILLIAN. (*Bitterly. Turning away and moving down* R.) That was nice of her. To make that a condition.

SHEP. Well, now I have, and I can get out of here. (*He starts to go, then stops.*) And, by the way, she's fixed it so you can't undo this one.

GILLIAN. (*Incensed.*) And how did she do that?

SHEP. How would I know? She pretended it was something she put into that disgusting mess she made me drink.

GILLIAN. I never heard such rubbish in all my life. For her to think that she could stop me like that. Oh, it's all right. I'll let you go. . . .

SHEP. You're damned right you will.

GILLIAN. But don't think that decision due to anything *she* did.

SHEP. We won't go into it—any of it. I've said what I had to say. (*He opens door.*)

GILLIAN. (*With an effort. She starts toward him.*) What about— Merle?

SHEP. What about her?

GILLIAN. Are you going back to her—if she'll have you?

SHEP. Right now the only thing I'm going to do is to get a couple of stiff drinks under my belt, and knock myself out. Forget the whole business—if I can . . . I'll say good night. (*He starts to go.*)

GILLIAN. (*Faintly.*) You mean—good-bye.

SHEP. Yes, I mean good-bye.

GILLIAN. (*Staring at him.*) I'll never see you again.

SHEP. I wouldn't know what for. (*He turns and goes. Offstage,* NICKY's *voice can be heard.*)

NICKY. (*Off.*) All through? (SHEP *does not answer.* NICKY *comes in, closes door and puts his coat on the bench.—Sunnily.*) Well? What cooks?

GILLIAN. You knew that's where he was.

NICKY. Yes, dear.

GILLIAN. That was your bright idea.

NICKY. (*Crossing to* R. *of sofa.*) No, darling, it was his. All his. He got Sid to call her up.

GILLIAN. (*Accepting this as justice. With sudden revulsion. She moves to back of* R. *chair.*) Oh, it's revolting! *His* getting mixed up with it. Going to see *her.* He's too good for that sort of thing.

NICKY. (*Protesting. He steps* R.) Now, wait a minute . .

GILLIAN. He is. It's cheapening to him. (*She crosses to below* C. *of coffee table.*) Scrabbling about in the gutters of the supernatural with Mrs. de Pass.

NICKY. (*Insinuatingly. He crosses* L. *of ottoman.*) Are you going to let her get away with it? Come on back to us, where you belong. Come to Natalie's party with me. (*There is a tap on the door. He opens it.* MISS HOLROYD *is outside.*)

MISS HOLROYD. Oh, Nicky—where's Gillian? (*She crosses to up* R. *of ottoman.*) Gillian, I've got Mr. Redlitch outside. (NICKY *closes door, comes back to below bookcase.*)

GILLIAN. Since when do you know Redlitch?

MISS HOLROYD. We met tonight at Mrs. de Pass'. And then we left together when Shep—went in. Will you see him? Just for a minute. It's important.

GILLIAN. I can't see anyone now.

MISS HOLROYD. Yes, but you see, it's about Shep and Mrs. de Pass. Mr. Redlitch is afraid you may be holding it against him.

GILLIAN. (*Turning slowly, letting her distress take itself out in anger. She stops to* L. *of coffee table.*) Oh, Yes—he took Shep up there, didn't he? All right, I'll see him.

MISS HOLROYD. I don't think you should be cross with him, darling.

GILLIAN. (*Coldly.*) Don't you? Bring him in.

MISS HOLROYD. Yes, dear. (MISS HOLROYD *goes out.*)

NICKY. Boy, will he need a drink! (*He goes into kitchen, puts on kitchen light.* MISS HOLROYD *comes back, followed by* REDLITCH.)

REDLITCH. (*Very conciliatory. He crosses to* L. *of ottoman.*) Good evening, Miss Holroyd. It's very nice of you to see me like this. (MISS HOLROYD *closes door and goes down to window seat.*)

GILLIAN. (*At* L. *of sofa.*) It's you I have to thank for taking Shep to Mrs. de Pass, haven't I, Mr. Redlitch? Taking him there to be cured of me.

REDLITCH. (*Crossing to down* L. *of ottoman.*) Oh, it wasn't that, Miss Holroyd.

GILLIAN. No? What was it, then?

REDLITCH. Well, it was—to put him back to where he was when he first met you. You know, like in Shakespeare . . . "Be as thou wast wont to be—See as thou wast wont to see." Midsummer Night's Dream, when they take off the power of the flower, and

GILLIAN. (*Finishing for him.*) And Titania falls out of love with the ass. Thank you for the comparison. (MISS HOLROYD *takes off her coat and gloves, puts them on window seat, crosses to* R. *chair and sits.*)

REDLITCH. Oh . . . Yes, I guess that was putting my foot in it. (NICKY *returns from kitchen, with a straight bourbon which he silently hands* REDLITCH, *who downs it hastily.* NICKY *crosses back to console.*) But—but what I want to explain is—*I* couldn't help myself. I figured at the time that you mightn't altogether like it . . .

GILLIAN. Oh, you did? Well, that was smart of you.

REDLITCH. And then when your aunt here told me you'd always had a hate on old Bianca . . .

GILLIAN. Bianca?

REDLITCH. Mrs. de Pass. Well, when I heard that—that you'd always been rivals, so to speak . . .

GILLIAN. (*Furious.*) We've never been rivals. That third-rate, vulgar, self-advertising, *mail-order* sorceress . . .

NICKY. Hey, take it easy, darling. She's about the best in the business. . . .

GILLIAN. (*Interrupting.*) It's people like her who make me wish we had the Inquisition back again. (*Crossing to* D.R. *of* MISS HOLROYD.) Do you know what she made him do? She made him come down here and tell me. Tell me what she'd done. Told him it was part of it. (REDLITCH *backs* L. *below sofa, puts his drink on table.*)

MISS HOLROYD. Well, maybe it is, dear.

GILLIAN. Not for anyone who knows their business. She can't be as bad at it as that. No, that was just to crow over me. (*Crossing* L. *above table to below sofa.*)

REDLITCH. (*During following speech* GILLIAN *crosses upstage around sofa to liquor console. As she walks* REDLITCH *turns to her, talking to her all the time.*) Look, Miss Holroyd, I don't know anything about that side of it. But I know you're no slouch yourself when it comes to revenge and that sort of thing. I don't want you to take it out on me. It was Shep's idea, the whole thing. All I did was take him there.

GILLIAN. (*Crossing to him.*) And now you're afraid of the consequences.

REDLITCH. (*Backing* L.) Well, only from you. I mean . . .

GILLIAN. (*Below* R. *of sofa.*) Why don't you ask Mrs. de Pass to protect you, if you think so highly of her? I'm sure she wouldn't consider a little thing like rendering me impotent beyond her powers. Or you might go to the local minister and get me exorcised —with Bell, Book and Candle.

REDLITCH. (*Backing to stove.*) Now listen, don't get mad. I haven't done anything, except what I was asked to do!

GILLIAN. (*Following him.*) Suppose you'd been asked to commit a murder. Or introduce someone to a murderer, who'd do the job for the sum of . . . (*Turns to* MISS HOLROYD.) Yes, what does she charge for a little chore like this?

MISS HOLROYD. Well, she varies her prices, dear. According to people's means. She asked me about Shep . . .

GILLIAN. And what did you tell her?

MISS HOLROYD. I told her I thought he was quite well off. You see, I'd seen his bank book, and letters from his broker . . .

NICKY. (*Comes to the back of* R. *chair.*) What did that set him back?

MISS HOLROYD. She said she was going to ask five thousand dollars.

GILLIAN. *What?*

MISS HOLROYD. Well, I thought it was a little high, but she did point out that—supposing you and he had been married, it would cost him a lot more than that to get divorced. . . .

GILLIAN. (*Crossing to up* R. *of sofa.*) Another pretty comparison.

REDLITCH. (*Crossing to below* C. *of sofa.*) Look, Miss Holroyd, I don't want to intrude on you in your—hour of grief, but—put yourself in my place.

GILLIAN. (*Turning to him, steps downstage.*) I'd rather not, Mr. Redlitch. But don't worry, I won't do anything to you.

REDLITCH. (*Crossing to her and shaking her hand.*) Gee, that's swell of you, Miss Holroyd. Thank you, thank you. (*Crossing below ottoman to* R. *of it.*) And—just one thing more. About the book. Nicky said you'd sort of—put a stopper on it. . . .

GILLIAN. Yes, I did.

REDLITCH. Well, don't you think—I mean, now that Shep's not— Oh—don't you think you might—I mean—well, sort of release it? (*Hastily.*) Oh, I don't mean right now—naturally. But some time when you've nothing else on your mind. . . . If you could just flip that off . . .

GILLIAN. (*Breaking in.*) Mr. Redlitch, don't you think from now on that you'd better stay clear of this kind of thing? I don't think you've got the temperament for it. Or the nerve, apparently.

REDLITCH. Maybe you're right. I only meant . . .

GILLIAN. Mr. Redlitch—*go away!* (*She crosses below sofa to stove.*)
REDLITCH. (*Crossing up to door, opens it.*) Oh, sure, sure. And thanks a lot, anyway. Good-bye. Good-bye, Miss Holroyd.
MISS HOLROYD. (*Going up to him, shaking hands.*) Good-bye. It was so nice meeting you. And . . . (*Intimately.*) I'll try and talk Gillian around about the book.
REDLITCH. Yeah, but—don't upset her. It's not worth it. Good-bye. (*He goes hurriedly.* MISS HOLROYD *closes door.*)
NICKY. (*Going to R. of sofa.* MISS HOLROYD *goes to back of R. table.*) Well, darling, how do you feel now?
GILLIAN. (*Inarticulate with rage, turns to him.*) Feel? Feel?
NICKY. Feel like coming to Natalie's party with me?
GILLIAN. (*Walking slowly below coffee table.*) Maybe. But I've got a little job to do here first.
NICKY. Old Bianca? (SHE *nods grimly. Crossing to* C.)
MISS HOLROYD. (*Crossing to back of R. chair.*) You know, you're wrong about her, Gillian. She was very nice about you tonight. She really was.
GILLIAN. (*Below ottoman.*) Yes, I'm sure she was. "Dear Gillian, I'm so fond of her. Just an amateur, of course, but really quite gifted in her way." Wasn't that it?
MISS HOLROYD. Well, sort of . . . Yes. But . . .
GILLIAN. (*Crossing above ottoman.*) Amateur. I'll show her.
NICKY. (*Backing down to coffee table.*) That's my little sister.
GILLIAN. (*During her next two speeches* GILLIAN *walks slowly around ottoman.*) She and her five thousand dollars. With her potions and her . . . I wondered why he said it tasted bad. I suppose she thought if it didn't, he wouldn't feel that he was getting his money's worth. It must have tasted revolting for that.
NICKY. (*Stepping to below sofa* L.) Maybe she gave him a candy, after.
GILLIAN. (*Below ottoman.*) It'll cost her a lot more than five thousand to get out of what I'll do to her. She's got a lot of valuable Chinese rugs, you once told me. And that mink coat! Well, we'll start with some moths! (*Crossing up to* R. C. *pillar.*)
MISS HOLROYD. (*Backing up to* R. *of table.*) Gillian, you mustn't.
GILLIAN. (*Crosses to* C.) Come to that, there's Merle, too. (*Furiously.*) "Be as Thou Wast Wont to Be." And how was that? In love with Merle Kittredge. No. She's not going to get him back. Not if I have anything to do with it. Where's Pyewacket? (*She opens kitchen door and calls.*) Pye—Pye—Pyewacket? Pye, where are

you? (*She goes into kitchen.*)

MISS HOLROYD. (*Crossing to above ottoman.*) I've never seen her like this before.

NICKY. (*Happily.*) Yes, but don't stop her.

GILLIAN. (*Returning.*) He's not there.

MISS HOLROYD. (*Crossing towards* GILLIAN.) Well, then, darling, why don't you wait and think it over till the morning?

GILLIAN. I can do without him. (*She goes to a closet in bookcase up* L. *and opens it.* NICKY *goes to up* L. *of sofa table.*) Let's see what I've got. (*She starts taking out bottles and looking at them.*)

MISS HOLROYD. (*Going towards* GILLIAN.) Darling, you can't have the moths in. Think of the other people in the building.

NICKY. (*Stepping downstage.*) Think of the moths!

GILLIAN. (*Muttering over labels.*) Where's that stuff I got in Haiti?

MISS HOLROYD. (*Going to* C.) And Merle . . . What are you going to do to her? Why don't you transport her somewhere?

GILLIAN. (*Still hunting.*) And have Shep go after her?

MISS HOLROYD. Then make her fall in love with someone else. Someone very unsuitable. (*Giggling.*) The garbage man, maybe.

GILLIAN. (*Takes out a small bottle.*) Here. Here we are. I've been waiting for an opportunity to try this.

NICKY. (*Crossing to* L. *of coffee table.*) What is it? (MISS HOLROYD *goes to above ottoman.*)

GILLIAN. (*Closing closet, going down to below sofa,* C.) Something really fancy. For revenges. Now, what have we got of theirs? (*To* MISS HOLROYD.) Do you have anything belonging to her?

MISS HOLROYD. To Mrs. de Pass? I've got her picture upstairs. But I don't think I should let you use that.

GILLIAN. (*Going to back of sofa table, gets pencil and two pieces of paper.*) I can write her name, and use that. That'll do. It'll also do for Miss Poison-Pen, too! (*Coming to below sofa* C., *sits.*)

NICKY. (*Crossing to* L. *of* GILLIAN.) This is a double-header. Quite a comeback you're staging.

MISS HOLROYD. (*Crossing to* R. *of sofa.*) Gillian, please, darling . . .

GILLIAN. Auntie, if you don't like it, you don't have to stay.

NICKY. (*Sits sofa* L.) Ah, let her see.

GILLIAN. Well, then, she must keep quiet. (*Writing.*) Bianca—eh? Has she any middle name?

MISS HOLROYD. I think it's Flo.

GILLIAN. (*Writing.*) Flo. De Pass. Good. (*She gets another sheet.*) Merle Emily Kittredge. Funny I should remember that it's Emily.

NICKY. Things do come back when they're needed.

GILLIAN. Put out the lights, Nicky. (HE *puts out all lights. Goes to console lamp, hall switch and sofa lamp. Then to* R. *of coffee table and kneels. The scene is now a repeat of the summoning of* RED-LITCH *in Act I.*) Auntie, the big ash tray.

MISS HOLROYD. (*Crossing to back of sofa table* L. *and timidly proffering it. She sits* L. *of* GILLIAN.) Here.

GILLIAN. Good. (*She settles. Crumples two papers into ash-tray. Takes a pinch of herbs from bottle and sprinkles them into ash-tray with paper. She mutters.*) Zaitux, Zorami, Elastot. . . . Got a match? (NICKY *produces some.* SHE *strikes a match, applies it to contents of ash-tray. It sputters and goes out.*) Damn. Another. (*She strikes another match. Same result.*) It won't light.

NICKY. The stuff must be old, or something.

GILLIAN. (*Scared.*) The paper won't light.

MISS HOLROYD. Maybe the ash-tray is damp.

GILLIAN. That wouldn't make any difference. I'll use the whole book this time. (*She strikes another match, then throws book of matches into tray and applies lighted match. Again it splutters and goes out.*) That's strange. . . . (*With sudden knowledge.*) Oh . . .! (*She switches on light.*)

NICKY. (*Arising.*) What is it?

GILLIAN. (*Rises.*) We're not going on with this.

NICKY. Why not?

GILLIAN. (*Going to above ottoman.*) I've changed my mind.

NICKY. (*Crossing to her.*) But, Gill . . .

GILLIAN. (*More firmly, crosses to* R. *of ottoman.*) I've changed my mind.

NICKY. (*Suspicious.*) There's nothing wrong, is there?

GILLIAN. No, no, of course not. You'd better go to your party, Nicky, I'll join you later. Nothing further is going to happen here tonight.

NICKY. (*Stepping* L.) Say, something really is wrong. You haven't been—defrosted, have you?

GILLIAN. No, of course not.

NICKY. Show me. Prove that.

GILLIAN. (*Moving away, going to below console, leaning against window arch.*) I'll do no such thing. I'm tired.

NICKY. (*After a pause.*) So, it is true, after all. The old wives' tales are true. Well, well, well! (*Crosses up to door and gets his coat.*) Let me hear from you some time, Gill. When you're feeling better, maybe? Good night. (*He goes out.*)

MISS HOLROYD. (*Rises.*) Gill, what is it?

GILLIAN. (*Returning to above ottoman* L.) Auntie—it *is* true.

MISS HOLROYD. You mean—you have lost your powers? You've fallen in love?

GILLIAN. I guess so. I guess it's happened to me.

MISS HOLROYD. With Shep, you mean?

GILLIAN. (*Angrily.*) Who else?

MISS HOLROYD. (*Sitting on sofa.*) Oh, but, darling—now—now . . .

GILLIAN. Yes, it's a fine time, isn't it? I've been coming down with it all evening. Only, I just didn't know what it was. (*Going to sofa, she sits* R. *end.*) Well, that's that. I guess I'm through. Through as a witch, anyway.

MISS HOLROYD. Gillian, what is love like? You know, I've never had it. Is it—wonderful?

GILLIAN. No—it's awful! (*She bursts into tears.*)

MISS HOLROYD. Oh, darling! Tears. Real tears.

GILLIAN. (*Weeping.*) Yes, and to think I've always envied people who *could* cry! It feels horrible! (*The tears turn into floods.*) Oh, Auntie, I don't *want* to be human—now! (*She sobs in* MISS HOLROYD'S *arms.*)

CURTAIN

ACT III

SCENE 2

Two months later.

Afternoon. All the objects savoring of witchcraft have been removed. There are flowers on R. *table, mantel and in a niche in bookcase. When the curtain rises,* NICKY *is discovered, trying to pour himself a drink at the liquor console. He finds whiskey bottle almost empty. He pours the last dregs from it, then tries door of console. It is locked. He snaps his fingers at it four times, tries it again, and it opens. He takes out a fresh bottle of Scotch and pours himself a drink. Buzzer sounds, and he answers it.*

NICKY. Hello?

MISS. HOLROYD'S VOICE. Is that Nicky? It's Aunt Queenie.

NICKY. Come on in. (*He buzzes her in, takes swallow of drink, and then closes console door, crosses* c., *turns back to it, snaps his fingers* [*to lock it*]. *Then opens door.* MISS HOLROYD *comes in, in a breathless fluster.*)

MISS HOLROYD. Nicky, dear—how nice. (*She kisses him.*) It's been such ages. Oh, I'm exhausted. Really, that 34th Street traffic. Nicky, you must teach me how to handle that. (*She crosses to sofa, puts her cape on it, and her gloves and bag on coffee table.*)

NICKY. (*Crossing to back of* R. *table.*) Yes, it's made you so late, I can't stay. (*He drinks.*)

MISS HOLROYD. (*Urgently—she crosses to ottoman.*) You must stay till Gillian gets here. That's why I got you here. You two can't go on this way. Especially when she's so unhappy.

NICKY. Is she still in love with Shep?

MISS HOLROYD. Yes, and he hasn't set foot in this building since that night.

NICKY. (*Crossing to* R. *of ottoman.*) What does Gill do with herself these days, anyway?

MISS HOLROYD. Well, she has a job.

NICKY. A job?

MISS HOLROYD. (*Sitting on ottoman.*) She goes to the movies. At first, she just went because they were a good place to cry in. And she said too, that if she was going to start having human emotions, she'd better learn something about them.

NICKY. From the movies?

MISS HOLROYD. Yes. And then one day she met a lady there whose job was seeing movies, and she asked Gillian if she'd like to do it, too. Gill sees two double features a day, and then reports on them. Writes them up in the evening.

NICKY. Wouldn't she rather be dead? (*He crosses to back of* R. *table, finishes drink and puts glass down.*)

MISS HOLROYD. Nicky, you mustn't say things like that. You must try to be kind.

NICKY. (*Crossing to her.*) Auntie, how can you, a self-respecting witch, say a thing like that?

MISS HOLROYD. (*As* NICKY *crosses above ottoman to sofa.*) Nicky, I don't want to scold you today, not about anything, but ever since your book died I understand you've been very discourteous to Sidney.

NICKY. (*Steps down.*) Sidney?

MISS HOLROYD. (*Coyly.*) You know—Mr. Redlitch.

NICKY. (*Amused.*) Hey, since when?

MISS HOLROYD. (*As before.*) Oh, quite a little while. We have dinner together every Wednesday. (*She rises, goes to up R. of ottoman.*)

NICKY. I didn't mean to be discourteous, but things have been pretty slim for me. (*He crosses up L.C. GILLIAN enters. She wears hat and coat.*)

GILLIAN. Auntie! Nicky! Oh, how nice. I haven't seen you since— well, not since. What brought you here? (*She embraces NICKY.*)

NICKY. I just thought I'd come around, and say hello. Or, rather, Aunt Queenie thought so.

GILLIAN. (*Crossing down to below sofa C.*) Oh, well, lovely. Come and sit down. (MISS HOLROYD *goes to back of R. chair.*)

NICKY. Look, I can't, today.

GILLIAN. (*Crossing up L. of sofa, puts her bag on table and her coat on sofa.*) Oh, just for a little. Won't you? Please, Nicky, please stay.

NICKY. (*Stepping down.*) I'm late as it is. I've got a date with Natalie. I'll come back some other time. I really will.

GILLIAN. All right.

NICKY. How's Pyewacket?

GILLIAN. He ran away.

NICKY. Because of . . . ?

GILLIAN. I guess so.

NICKY. Nothing for him to do around here any more? (*He looks at her.*) You know, Gill, you *look* different. I don't know *how,* exactly, but . . .

GILLIAN. Better or worse?

NICKY. That depends upon your taste, I guess. Good-bye, Gill. (*He crosses up C., picks up his coat.*) Good-bye, Auntie. (*He goes.*)

MISS HOLROYD. (*Stepping L.*) What did you see this afternoon, dear?

GILLIAN. I didn't stay. They were two comedies.

MISS HOLROYD. You're very nervous.

GILLIAN. (*With a sudden intensity.*) Auntie . . . Shep's upstairs! (*She crosses to L. of coffee table.*)

MISS HOLROYD. (*Crossing up R. of ottoman.*) Oh, darling, how do you know?

GILLIAN. (*Crossing to down C.*) I saw him at his window. Just a flash of him.

MISS HOLROYD. (*Going to R. of sofa.*) Did he see you?

GILLIAN. (*Crossing to up L. of R. chair.*) I don't know. I'm afraid he may have.

MISS HOLROYD. Not afraid!

GILLIAN. I've been so thankful that he's not been in the place—that

I've not bumped into him. And now, the feeling that he's just up there is more than I can stand. (*Going to* R. *of ottoman.*) Let's not have dinner here. (*Panicking.*) Let's go out. Let's go out right now!

MISS HOLROYD. (*Firmly.*) No. I wish I could summon him.

GILLIAN. Summon him?

MISS HOLROYD. Yes, then we could tell him what's happened to you. About your—accident. And what caused it.

GILLIAN. (*Crossing to above* R. *table.*) Tell him? I'd go to any lengths to stop his finding out.

MISS HOLROYD. But, darling, why?

GILLIAN. Something called pride, I guess. Or shame. You know, they're new emotions to me. Or else they're very old ones, in reverse. The other side of the coin. (*A knock on the door.* SHE *retreats a step, startled.*)

MISS HOLROYD. (*Crossing up.*) Oh, it's him! (*Correcting herself.*) It's he!

GILLIAN. (*Distracted, crossing to her.*) It can't be! Help me. Open the door, but don't leave me. Promise. (*Knock is repeated.* MISS HOLROYD *goes to door.* GILLIAN *goes to below sofa. She opens it.* SHEP *is standing outside. He carries a suitcase.*)

SHEP. (*Coming in.*) Hello.

MISS HOLROYD. Hello, Shep. (*Closes door.*)

SHEP. (*To* GILLIAN.) Are you busy, or could I see you for a moment?

GILLIAN. I have Aunt Queenie here.

MISS HOLROYD. (*To* GILLIAN, *going to sofa* R.) Darling. I'm going to run along. I have a dinner engagement. (*She gets her cape, gloves and bag.*)

GILLIAN. (*Steps to her.*) But I thought we . . .

MISS HOLROYD. (*Backing up* C.) No, darling. I forgot to tell you. But I'll call you. Later. See? Good-bye, Shep. It's so lovely you dropped in! (*She goes.*)

SHEP. (*Steps down.*) I'm afraid Miss Holroyd has the wrong idea of what I came here for. This isn't a friendly visit.

GILLIAN. I didn't imagine that it was.

SHEP. (*Puts his suitcase down* R. *of door.*) I'm leaving for Europe and I came down here to get some things I needed. (*Indignantly.*) I've only just discovered that I still have an apartment here. I told my secretary right after—that night—to move me the hell out of here and never mention the place to me again. (*Going to above ottoman. Belatedly.*) I don't mean to be offensive.

GILLIAN. I understand.

SHEP. Today I found my stuff is not in storage at all. I'm stuck with this place. No sublet. You can't expect me to believe nowadays there are suddenly no tenants to be had. I see your hand in this, and I don't intend to put up with it. (*Steps to down* R. *of sofa.*)

GILLIAN. (*Steps* R.) What have I done?

SHEP. You know damn well what you've done. Fixed it that way.

GILLIAN. What did the agents tell your secretary?

SHEP. I don't know what they told her. I didn't let her get that far. I intend to deal with this, myself.

GILLIAN. I see. You mean—deal with me. I can't do anything about it.

SHEP. You mean, you won't.

GILLIAN. If it will end this interview, I'll accept that. (*She turns away* L. *to stove.*)

SHEP. (*Stepping down* L.) But I won't accept it. This is sheer vindictiveness. Trying to hold me here.

GILLIAN. (*Bursting out. Turns and crosses toward him.*) And I won't accept that. The whole thing is in your lease, as you could have found out if you'd been willing to look or listen, instead of jumping to insane conclusions. The owner here won't let me give a sublet clause. And if you think I fixed that, in some way or other, I'll dispel that illusion, too. I don't want you in this house. I'd far rather you were out of it. And I'll make that clear by canceling your lease, if that will suit you.

SHEP. You will?

GILLIAN. Gladly.

SHEP. Done.

GILLIAN. Good.

SHEP. Fine!

GILLIAN. Finished! (*She goes to stove,* SHEP *goes up to door.*)

SHEP. (*Picking up suitcase, glancing at his watch.*) Oh . . .

GILLIAN. What is it?

SHEP. I was just wondering if my secretary would still be in the office.

GILLIAN. Do you want to call and see?

SHEP. (*Eyeing phone, half-humorously.*) On that phone?

GILLIAN. Well, if you prefer not to . . .

SHEP. It's not my favorite telephone. But I'll take a chance. (*Puts his suitcase and hat* R. *of door. He goes to it, and dials.* GILLIAN *goes down* R. *to window seat, sits.*) I'm sorry I got sore.

GILLIAN. I did, too.

SHEP. (*Forcing friendliness.*) How have you been?

GILLIAN. (*Doing likewise.*) Fine. And you?

SHEP. Fine. How's Pyewacket?

GILLIAN. He . . . (*She checks herself.*) He's fine.

SHEP. Keeping busy?

GILLIAN. Him or me?

SHEP. Both of you. (*He answers phone.*) Hello . . . Miss Bishop? I'm sorry I flew off the handle. I'm at Miss Holroyd's apartment. I've arranged to cancel the lease. Will you look after it? I won't be in the office in the morning, so why don't I leave the key here? With Miss Holroyd. Then you can get it from her. (*To* GILLIAN.) Is that all right?

GILLIAN. Certainly.

SHEP. (*Into phone.*) Okay, then. What? What rent? Well, haven't you been . . . ? Well, why not? All right. All right. I'll deal with it. Good-bye. (*He hangs up, crosses to* L. *of ottoman.*) I gather I owe you some rent. Three months, to be exact.

GILLIAN. (*Going to* R. *of* R. *table.*) No. No, you don't.

SHEP. Why not?

GILLIAN. I owe you far more than that.

SHEP. What do you owe me?

GILLIAN. Well—well, five thousand dollars, anyway.

SHEP. Huh?

GILLIAN. That Mrs. de Pass charged you. That was outrageous.

SHEP. I thought it was a bit excessive, myself. But I'd nothing to compare it with.

GILLIAN. I wish that I could pay it. I ought to, I know. But I can't. (*Turns* R.)

SHEP. I don't see that it's your responsibility. But thanks for thinking of it. Do you mind if I leave a note for my secretary? She's terribly dumb. (*He goes to back of sofa table.*)

GILLIAN. (*Very tentatively.*) How is it—going? I mean—how's Merle?

SHEP. (*After a tiny pause.*) She's fine—I guess.

GILLIAN. (*Turning to him, crossing to above* R. *chair.*) You—guess? Didn't you—go back to her? Or was that spoiled?

SHEP. (*Unwillingly.*) No, I went back to her.

GILLIAN. And then what happened? I'm sorry to be inquisitive, but it has been rather like—not knowing the end of a movie.

SHEP. Yes, I can see that. Well, I went back, but—it didn't work.

GILLIAN. Because of me? What did you tell her about me?

SHEP. Nothing.

GILLIAN. (*Steps* L.) Didn't she want to know? How you had come to leave her?

SHEP. Yes, but I wouldn't go into it. Beyond the fact that I'd been—well, "bewitched" was the word I used. (GILLIAN *turns away.*) I didn't say I meant it literally. And then—something happened. Something she had done. I can't tell you what, but—it finished things.

GILLIAN. (*Turning* R.) It wasn't—a letter? An anonymous letter, was it?

SHEP. (*Surprised, he walks to up* L. *of ottoman.*) What makes you ask that? Was that a habit of hers?

GILLIAN. I'm afraid it was.

SHEP. Actually, it was a letter she had written to my partner while I was—with you.

GILLIAN. Oh, yes, you said he had been acting strangely.

SHEP. That was why.

GILLIAN. (*Genuinely.*) I'm sorry. Very sorry. (*She crosses* L. *to below* L. *of coffee table.*)

SHEP. You know, this is odd—for you.

GILLIAN. What is?

SHEP. (*Crossing to* R. *of coffee table.*) All this—interest. This curiosity . . . You look different, too.

GILLIAN. (*Scared.*) How—different? (*She goes to stove* L.)

SHEP. I don't know. But something about you. (*Looking* R. *and back to her.*) There's something about this place, too.

GILLIAN. (*Hastily.*) I've changed some things in the apartment. That's all the difference is. (*Eager to end interview, she crosses to* L. *of coffee table.*) And—look, please, you don't have to stay and be polite.

SHEP. Yes, I have got a great deal to do. . . . (*He makes a move, then stops, remembering something.*) Oh—my key. (*He takes a single key from his pocket. Goes up to sofa table. Gets note.*) Will you give it to my secretary? (*He hands them to her.*)

GILLIAN. (*Stepping in, taking it.*) Of course.

SHEP. (*Steps* R.—*stops; awkwardly.*) And that reminds me. There's something else. I've been wondering how I could go about returning it. (*Pause.*) It's the key to—this apartment. (*He takes out his key-ring.*)

GILLIAN. (*Turning away.*) Will you excuse me for a moment. (*She goes swiftly into bedroom.* SHEP *looks after her, surprised by the suddenness of her exit. Then he takes key off ring and goes to* R. *of sofa table.* GILLIAN *returns, carrying something in her hand.*)

SHEP. (*Holding out key to her.*) Here.

GILLIAN. (*At L. of sofa table. Unwilling to touch it.*) Put it down, will you? (HE *does so. There is a tiny pause. Then, with equal embarrassment.*) I've been wondering how I could go about returning this to you.

SHEP. What is it?

GILLIAN. Your locket.

SHEP. I gave you that.

GILLIAN. Under false pretenses. I've felt worse about having that, than over anything. Like a thief. Please take it.

SHEP. It doesn't mean that much.

GILLIAN. It does to me. Please.

SHEP. Very well, then. (*She drops it in his hand. He looks at it, then slips it into his pocket.*)

GILLIAN. I feel better. And now, I think I'd like you to go. (*She crosses down R. to below R. chair.*)

SHEP. (*Slowly.*) Yes . . . Yes . . . (*He stands, looking at her.*)

GILLIAN. Don't stare at me. Please go. (*She turns front.*)

SHEP. (*Continuing to stare. He goes up to suitcase, then crosses to down R. of R. table.*) It's strange to look at you like this. The way I see you now is like a kind of—double image. Someone who's completely new and strange—and someone I've know intimately. (*With implication.*) *Very* intimately. It would be hard to forget that. Here, especially. (*She turns away.*)

GILLIAN. (*With her back to him.*) Do you mind going?

SHEP. (*Goes to her, back of table. She averts her face.*) Gill—you're not blushing?

GILLIAN. No, of course I'm not. (*She struggles to keep her head turned away.*)

SHEP. (*Steps L.*) You're crying, too.

GILLIAN. (*Angrily, backing down L.*) All right, then, I'm crying!

SHEP. But I thought . . .

GILLIAN. (*Crossing above ottoman and below sofa to stove.*) You thought we couldn't—didn't you? Well, you were wrong!

SHEP. (*Slowly, going to above ottoman.*) Are you quite sure of that?

GILLIAN. Quite sure.

SHEP. (*Stepping L.*) Well, I'm not! You're different. You're completely different. Why?

GILLIAN. What does it matter?

SHEP. It matters to me. One hell of a lot! (*Going to R. of sofa.*) Tell me—are you—not one, any more? It that it? (*Goes to her, takes her by shoulders.*) Is it? I've got to know.

GILLIAN. (*Turning, violently, steps back.*) All right, then. I have lost my powers. Now you do know. I guess you're entitled to that much satisfaction. (*Crossing* R. *below coffee table.*) And now will you please leave me alone?

SHEP. (*After a beat, quietly.*) How did you lose them?

GILLIAN. (*Up* C., R. *of ottoman.*) They just—went.

SHEP. (*Going to below coffee table, following her.*) Is that apt to happen?

GILLIAN. (*Up* L. *of* R. *chair. Shortly.*) Under certain circumstances.

SHEP. What circumstances?

GILLIAN. There are all kinds.

SHEP. (*Forcibly, going to her, takes her hand.*) No, there's only one way. It was in that book of Redlitch's.

GILLIAN. Redlitch doesn't know anything about it.

SHEP. But Nicky does. And he helped write it.

GILLIAN. (*She breaks away to up* R. *of* R. *chair, her back to him. Desperately.*) Shep, if you've ever had any regard for me, please go now. What's the point in going on at me like this?

SHEP. (*He backs to above ottoman. Slowly.*) Because something has been happening since I came into this room. I want to be sure that it's the real thing—this time. (*She looks up at him, getting his meaning. Her face begins to shine with an incredulous rapture.* SHEP *smiles, then moves.*) I *will* go now. (*He picks up his hat and suitcase. She stands staring at him, bewildered, dazed. He comes back into room, above ottoman.*) And maybe I won't go to Europe—just yet. I'd like to give those images a chance to blend. (*Smiling, teasingly.*) I suppose you have got some idea of what I'm talking about?

GILLIAN. (*Slowly.*) I—think so. It's been happening to me, too—for —such a long time.

SHEP. (*Gently, smilingly.*) It has?

GILLIAN. (*In a small voice.*) I'm only human! (*He sets down suitcase and his hat on ottoman. They are in the same spot as at the end of the first scene of Act I. Slowly, as before, they move toward each other, ending, in each other's arms.*)

CURTAIN

SCENE DESIGN

"BELL, BOOK & CANDLE"

DESIGNED BY
GEORGE JENKINS

71

Window-curtains, Drapes & Shutters—*OPEN*
Window Seat—4 Christmas Packages
Liquor Console—Liquor Tray
   1 Bottle of Scotch
   1 Bottle of Bourbon
   6 Old-fashioned glasses
   3 Martini glasses
   1 Full bottle of Scotch in Cupboard
Water Pitcher (full)
Ice-Bucket
Tongs
Bottle Opener
Bottle of Soda (small)
Side Table—
   Ash-Tray
   Cigarette Box
   Lighter
   Scissors (in drawer)
Christmas Tree Table—Christmas Tree, Decorations—Lights
   On Shelf—2 Christmas packages (records)
         6 other packages variously decorated
Book-Case—
   Drawing of Brazilian Dancer—R. of Bookcase
   Manual in Cupboard
   Various bottles, phials, etc.—in cupboard
   1 framed drawing—R. of bedroom
Sofa Table—R. *End*—Phone
   1 small ash-tray (Above phone)
   1 cast iron tray—C.
   Large ash-tray with *Flame Effect*—L. end
   Cigarette cup and Lighter
   Phone Pad and Pencil (R. end)
   Fountain Pen (behind lamp)
   Waste-Basket (*Under* R. *End*)
   1 lamp—L. end
Sofa—2 Pillows—either end
Coffee Table—
   Ash-Tray
   Cigarette cup with cigarettes and kitchen matches

Lighter
Pack of matches
2 African face cup
1 coal box with coal shovel and coal—down L.
Ottoman—Down c.
Flame effect: 1 fuse with two kitchen matches taped to it at point of contact. Small round receptacle in c. of the ashtray with alcohol and absorbent cotton. Magnesium powder is spread on the end of the fuse and around the outside of the alcohol receptacle.
On Mantel:
Upper end—1 brass bird on wooden base
c.—small Mexican twin pottery piece
Lower end—1 small carved black African fetish
On Lower Mantel: 1 heavy brass mortar and pestle on black wooden base
Small stove.
Above Stove: 1 fire set
In Bookcases:
1 clay horse on second shelf from top
1 red leather round shield, 1 carved African goddess on a black wooden base—in large R. niche
On Top c. Panel of bookcase—1 Cabal picture
Above bedroom door—1 witch ball
2 paintings on Kitchen Door
4 different sized paintings on wall, R. of liquor console, 3 on wall above it
Various paintings and objets d'art above bookcases and mantel
Pre-set in Kitchen
Martini Pitcher—(Full)
Tea tray with doily—2 cups, saucers, spoons ⎫
  Sugar Bowl with Cube Sugar   ⎬ *Act II*
Tea-Pot
1 old-Fashioned Glass with Liquor ⎫
Pitcher of Water and Glasses   ⎬ *Act III*
Pre-set in Bedroom—L.
Pitcher of water and glasses
Locket—*Act III*
Pre-set Off R.
SHEP   2 small Christmas Packages
         Carton of Christmas Packages including LOCKET in jewelry box

73

	Small Diary and Pencil	
	Keys on Key Ring (1 separate key)	
	Suitcase	
GILLIAN	Box of Candy	Back c.
	4 Letters (unopened)	
QUEENIE	2 Christmas Packages (2 Books) with white wrappings	
	1 other Christmas Package	
NICKY	2 Christmas Packages—(Unguent Jar, and Phial)	
	Manuscript in Envelope—*Act II*	

SCENE CHANGES

Act I—Scene 2
Strike: On coffee Table—
  African Cup
  Wrapping paper
  Phial
  Flame Ash-tray
Re-set:
to R. end:
  Ash-tray
  Lighter
  Cigarette holder and matches
Set: On Window Seat:
  Shep's coat (upper seat)
  Gill's jacket—above Shep's coat
  Carton of gifts (below coat)
  Hat and muffler—on coat
  Books, records, wrappings—below carton
Strike:
  On Liquor Console: Martini glasses and Pitcher
Strike:
  On Table R.: wrapping paper, book
Re-set: scissors in drawer
Shutters—*Closed*
Bedroom door—Open

Act II
Strike: On Window Seat: Carton, books, gifts, wrappings
Strike: On U.L. bookshelf: 2 drawings (Mat, and framed)
Strike: Christmas tree, table, gifts. Liquor glass—on coffee table
Strike: Liquor Tray

Re-Set: Pillows on sofa
Re-Set: *On Sofa Table:*
  big ash-tray to R. end
  phone to L. end
  smaller ash-tray to L. end
Re-Set: *On Coffee Table:*
  Ash-tray, lighter, cig. holder—L.C.
Re-Set: Ottoman to 6 inches up c.
Set: *On Wall* U.R.C.:
  Mexican Mask
  Lacquer & cane chair below it.
Drapes—Curtains—*OPEN*
Doors—*CLOSED*
Shutters—*OPEN*
Check: Ash-trays, Cigarettes in all containers

Act III—Scene 1
Strike: Mexican Mask
        4 Letters (2 on c. table, 2 on s. table)
        Glass in kitchen
Re-Set: *Phone* to R. end of Sofa Table
        Big Ash-tray to L. end of sofa table
        Smaller Ash-tray to R. end of sofa table (above phone)
Drapes—*OPEN*
All doors—*CLOSED*
CLOSE—Coal Box
Check: all ash-trays (big one—wet)
       Cigarettes in all containers
Check: Locket—Off L.
Fill bottle of Scotch
Re-set in console drawer
Set: Mask (broken)—1 part on R. chair. The other part on floor, down L. of chair.

Scene 2
Strike: Brass Bird and African god—on mantel
Strike: Witch Ball—above bedroom door
Strike: 2 pieces of mask—on sofa table
Strike: Box of candy—on R. table
Strike: Mortar and Pestle—on lower mantel
Strike: Mexican Horse—on 3rd bookshelf to behind books on same shelf

Strike: Liquor glass, large ash-tray—on coffee table
Strike: Shield, base and African goddess—from bookshelf niche
Set: Two ivy plants in yellow metal containers—on either side of the mantel
Set: Brass pitcher with yellow jonquils—on lower mantel
Set: Cast iron bracket with potted ivy—on wall L. of kitchen door
Set: Pot of white azaleas—in niche
Set: Liquor tray as in Act I—with 4 glasses and almost empty Scotch bottle (no Bourbon)—1 glass partly filled
Re-Set: Gold pencil—from coffee table to sofa table
Herb jar—to closet in bookshelf
Reverse: Cabalistic painting on top c. of bookshelves
Set: China mug in niche where Mexican horse was
Close: White drapes
All doors